Every Time
I Turn Around,
God Whispers In My Ear!

WHAT OTHERS ARE SAYING ABOUT

EVERY TIME I TURN AROUND, GOD WHISPERS IN MY EAR!

At a time when many are confused about their value and identity, Barb Boswell reminds readers that whether they are broken or battered, God will meet them where they are. A gifted storyteller, with a healthy dose of humor, Barb calls believers back to the heart of the Father to find love and restoration. *Every Time I Turn Around, God Whispers in My Ear!* is timely, powerful, and beautiful.

—Georgene Rice, host of the Georgene Rice Show Musician and coauthor of *Undaunted, The Daring Journey of Faith*

Barb has been one of my favorite authors and speakers for years, but this book, *Every Time I Turn Around, God Whispers in My Ear!* scores a homerun for me. Just as Jesus spoke stories to drive home a spiritual truth, Barb perfectly articulates her life experiences through the lens of God's love. I put down the book after each chapter and pause; wondering why we so complicate our faith. This book will bring a smile to your heart, a lift in your step, and a fire to your faith. All I want to say is, "More!"

—Erin Campbell Erin Campbell Ministries, Cincinnati, Ohio

Barb writes as if she were chatting with you from an armchair in your living room, coffee cup in hand. Her stories are based on a life that is just like yours and mine, and her words are powerful because they are simple. Simple enough to be real. Simple enough to be relevant. Simple enough to be able to encourage readers wherever they find themselves in life. This book will allow you to laugh as well as be challenged about the way you see yourself and God. A perfect devotional or discussion starter for women who want to have their hearts refocused on Him in the middle of their everyday lives.

—**Kim Lawson, East Park Church, Vancouver, Washington**

Barb Boswell has once again combined her humor, humanness, and wisdom to write her captivating third book, *Every Time I Turn Around, God Whispers in My Ear!* She continues the journey of bumping into God, catching glimpses of God, and now hearing Him.

I love that Barb the author is as authentic as Barb the friend...an everyday person. I know that you will enjoy this book as much as I have and just maybe you will hear God whisper in your ear. Listen for Him!

—**Rachel Eggum Cinader**
President of Hope 4 Women International

She's at it again! *Every Time I Turn Around, God Whispers in My Ear!* will be an incredible encouragement for your faith and Christian walk. Barb brings unique insight through her creative and practical way of saying things. If you want a boost in your faith and a dash of encouragement, pick up this book. It is sure to be a breath of fresh air to your life!

—**Pastor Len Ballenger**
Jubilee International Ministries, Pensacola, Florida

The first time I "met" Barb was over the phone. My husband and I had moved from New York to host a morning radio show in Portland, Oregon. My husband was always referencing the Yankees on the show. One day Barb called to inform him that he was now on the West Coast, and he needed a new hat, preferably a Mariners' hat, Barb's favorite team. Maybe it was Barb's deadpan approach, or simply the tone of her voice, but I remember releasing one of those delightful, deep, howling belly laughs. A friendship was born. As we got to know Barb and discovered her books, I realized that her writing was peppered with the same well-developed sense of humor and sharp wit that we had experienced during our initial "meeting." So when Barb's latest book, *Every Time I Turn Around, God Whispers in My Ear!* began with her sharing thoughts about being in a deep dark valley and losing joy, I was intrigued. Having shared the company of "Pharisees and Sadducees," myself, I wanted to know, "What did Barb do? How did she overcome the challenges?" Once again, I experienced the joyful medicine of reading a Barb Boswell book, resplendent with her trademark ability to perceive the humor in a situation, even under the most adverse circumstances.

—**Brenda Bissett-Steinhofer, Radio Personality**
"Pete & Brenda in the Morning"
past: WASH-FM, WSB-FM, WPOC-FM, WCAO

As a mother and grandmother I took great delight in the stories, and especially the ones involving life lessons learned from our very own children and grandchildren. "Damaged Goods" in particular struck a chord with me, having been through something similar with one of my sons. Best of all, the stories don't leave you hanging, there's always a fitting follow up verse(s) that await. Very well written.

—**Corry Reynolds, Radio Personality and Author**

Over the years, Barb and I have exchanged professional ideas about book publishing and ministry. Somehow, she brings out the fun in life. One would never know she went through rough times in her life. She always seems to bounce back up (with help from her sense of humor) and land on her feet, walking with Jesus hand in hand. I recommend her new book as she is vulnerable and transparent, helping the reader connect with a real person. This allows the reader to trust her and walk this journey together. Thank you, Barb, for being you. I admire and respect you greatly. May the Lord continue to use you for His glory wherever you go.

—**Pastor Kris Belfils, Hope Fellowship, Spokane, Washington**
Author of *The Garbage Man Always Comes on Fridays*

Barb and I have served alongside one another in ministry and I consider her a good friend. I have always appreciated her ability to connect the "messiness" of daily life with the timeless words of Scripture. Barb has a gift for connecting with those she speaks to and those she writes for whether the topic is parenting, baseball, or the struggle within us to see ourselves as worthy of God's love. For all those seeking a genuine walk with God that encompasses daily joys and struggles, you'll find Barb's latest book a welcome companion. I am thankful that Barb has shared her reflections on those things God has whispered in her ear and has invited us into the conversation she keeps with her Lord and Savior.

—**Pastor Chris Haughee**
Chaplain, Intermountain Children's Home, Helena, Montana
(intermountainministry.org)

"Turbo" Barb volunteers many times a year at Cannon Beach Christian Conference Center. During each visit to CBCC, Barb shares a morning devotion with our group of volunteers from her personal life journey... some of encouragement and some of struggles...always giving glory to God. These devotions, experiences, and stories are the essence of *Every Time I Turn Around, God Whispers in My Ear!* Thank you, Barb, for so candidly sharing your life with us.

—Jean Hand
Cannon Beach Conference Center (Oregon) Volunteer Coordinator

Barb and I met at a large booksellers' convention in Orlando, Florida. I was feeling lost and alone, and a bit homesick. I prayed for a friend and met Barb at a table at a snack bar. She shared her journey and some of her writing with me. In her words, spoken and on the page, she touched my heart.

I've read her books and have given them to others. They are all excellent, but *Every Time I Turn Around, God Whispers in My Ear!* is her best yet. Her writing is courageous, honest, and genuine. She loves God in the storms of life and hears Him there...even when it's hard, chaotic, and down-right painful.

I came to this book ready to hear Him through her writing. And I did. I highly recommend all of Barb's books, especially this one. Her words made me laugh. I cried, and a few times I said, "Yeah, I get that!" out loud. And there was more than one "Amen!"

—Joy DeKok, author of *Rain Dance*

I connected with Barb at an American Cancer Society Board of Directors dinner. I had just lost my mother to lung cancer and was on my own personal search to connect further with Jesus. Barb shared with me that she was a cancer survivor. She also shared her love for Jesus with me. This was all prior to her first book being published. She has remained my inspiration and guiding light as, together, we continue to fight for a cure for cancer. More recently, Barb was my encouragement to share my faith publicly during a time when God orchestrated a miracle that saved my son's life. Barb is an inspiration to many as she shares her Jesus and her cancer story as she speaks to cancer survivors at Relay for Life events around the county. You will find the words in this book come from her heart and they are guaranteed to make you stop and think about your own relationship with Jesus.

—**Marilyn Dryke**
Friend and Relay for Life Leader, Vancouver, Washington

While visiting the USA in 2000, Barb and I met through a mutual friend. At that time Barb was in the throes of writing her first book, *Every Time I Turn Around, I Bump into God!* Since then her second book has been published and now, a third book. She will show you that her Jesus is truly alive and wants to be an active participant in our lives, if we would only let Him. Barb's encounters with her Lord, have given her a rich knowledge of who Jesus is, how He works, and it is her desire that each of her readers may know this same Jesus in the way as she does. Every circumstance that she has journeyed through has been a testament of faith in the God whom she has learned to "Trust and Obey."

—**Elizabeth Kay, Australia Alumni, Mercy Ships Volunteer**

Every Time
I Turn Around,
God Whispers In My Ear!

Barb Boswell

EVERY TIME I TURN AROUND, GOD WHISPERS IN MY EAR!

Unless otherwise indicated, all Scripture quotations are taken from the *Holy Bible*, New Living Translation, copyright © 1996. Used by permission of Tyndale House Publishers, Inc., Wheaton, Illinois 60189. All rights reserved.

Scripture quotations marked NIV are taken from the HOLY BIBLE, NEW INTERNA-TIONAL VERSION. Copyright © 1973, 1978, 1984 International Bible Society. All rights reserved throughout the world. Used by permission of Zondervan Bible Publishers.

Scripture quotations marked MSG are taken from *The Message*. Copyright © 1993, 1994, 1995, 1996, 2000, 2001, 2002. Used by permission of NavPress Publishing Group.

All italics have been added by the author for emphasis in quoted Scripture passages.

ISBN-10: 0-692-69168-5

ISBN-13: 978-0-692-69168-7

Printed by Gorham Printing, Centralia, WA 98531 www.gorhamprinting.com
Edited by Sue Miholer of Picky, Picky Ink

Cover design by Marlece Pierce, Tactile Graphics www.tactilegraphicsonline.com
Author photo by Joannrenee Photography joannreneephotography@gmail.com

For Clara and Renee,

My beautiful and precious granddaughters.
I love you to infinity.

Grandma

CONTENTS

ACKNOWLEDGMENTS

Welcome back friends. It's been a long time since we've connected. Life for me since my second book was published in 2007 has had its ups and down, highs and lows and gains and losses. Yet the one constant in my life has been my unwavering faith in Jesus Christ. Some of the stories in this book were extremely difficult to write. They poured out of a disappointed and discouraged heart. I couldn't have written those three years ago, or even last year, without sounding bitter and accusing. I'm not bitter; I'm better. God has a way of turning our ashes into beauty. There were times, like in the psalms of David where he shook his fist at God, and by the end of the psalm, David was praising Him. That was me. God has been continually pursuing me, even during those times when I didn't pursue Him. Oh how He loves us!

Many have encouraged me to continue with my writing journey. Many have said, "I have your two books. When is the next one coming out?" I would sigh and think never, while in my mind I kept hearing this *loud* whisper..."do it!" And so, we have what I would call the third book in the series. My first book, *Every Time I Turn Around, I Bump into God!* was published after much encouragement, even though I went kicking and screaming into the process. Book two, *Every Time I Turn Around, I Catch a Glimpse of God!* followed. I wasn't as reluctant this time. Now, here we are with *Every Time I Turn Around, God Whispers in My Ear!* We bump into Him, we catch glimpses of Him and now, He speaks to us—all in the daily-ness of life. As depicted on the cover of this book, you can see how I react when God "whispers." I put my hands over my ears and make loud humming noises, trying to drown out His voice. Let me tell you, it doesn't work.

You will hear a common theme in the stories that follow: Be still, listen, focus. I was finally able to write some of these stories because the pain had subsided. Some stories took years to be able to write. I questioned how God could be found in "those" years. My prayer is that you will find joy in the journey and healing in the pain, realizing God is always there, in the good and bad times. You will also experience a common verse throughout these stories from 1 Kings 19:11–12. There is a lot of clutter and clamoring going on in this world today. I encourage you to cover your ears. Don't listen to what the world throws at you. Listen for the voice of God! Listen with your heart.

Who do I thank for going along on this journey with me? There are so many of you.

To my family, for putting up with me. Yes, you do provide the subject matter for many of these stories. Not sure if a thank you or apology is in order. Thank you, Ron, for helping me move boxes of books, again and again.

To my P.I.C. (partner in Christ or crime), aka my best and dearest friend, Carol McCallum. You have been a loyal friend, sticking closer than a sister and encouraging me to write this book. Sometimes the encouragement didn't *sound* like encouragement to my ears, but it did to my heart. You wear many hats in my life: friend, business advisor, fashion consultant, event assistant and traveling companion. We *do* have fun! Thank you for staying by my side when others walked out.

A special shout out to my "groupie" trio: Lisi, Skye, and L.B. You've sat through many of my speaking events, hearing me speak so many times that any one of you could fill in for me!

To my daughter-in-law Joann Boswell, mother of my two precious granddaughters, who has an extraordinary eye for photography. Thank you for taking the picture on the back cover and making me look presentable—squinty eyes and all.

To Sue Miholer, my editor and friend. Thanks for keeping my voice in these chapters and for your pre-book advice.

To Barb and Cal Schurman. Many stories in the book were written at your house at Hood Canal. I am forever grateful. Enjoy living there full time!

And to all of my friends, near and far, who said, "When is the next book coming out?" I appreciate your encouragement, even though I sighed when you asked.

Above all, I thank my Lord and Savior Jesus Christ. I am nothing without You. All the glory, honor and praise goes to You.

FOREWORD

When Barb approached me about writing the foreword for her new book, I tossed aside the doubts and eagerly said yes. I am thrilled to introduce you, the reader, to someone whom I respect as a woman who honors God in her day-to-day life.

More than 50 years ago, as new Christians, my husband and I were approached by our church to lead the ninth-grade youth group. In our eagerness to be "good" Christians, we said yes—but with no idea what to do with them. Our first couple of meetings were so bad that even the original six "church" kids were begging their folks to let them "not go."

We prayed for answers, knowing it was going to take activities and food to get more "niners" to attend. Our merry band of six was challenged to invite a friend or two and the Lord began to increase our numbers.

We started planning a winter ski retreat. One of our rules was that if you wanted to attend the retreats, the "fun stuff," you had to be involved in the weekly youth group night. Enter Barb's good friend Alice, who mentioned to Barb that she was going on a weekend ski retreat and "do you want to go?" Now Barb was one heck of a successful athlete and sooooo wanted to go skiing, but that church thing...not so much!

The enticement of a ski weekend won out and she showed up for youth group. My first observation was she was a "mini-me," a reflection of myself at that age—angry, lonely, withdrawn, not trusting of any adult (no matter how "cool" I was). She sat on the fringe of our gathering, looking for any reason to bolt like a scared and wounded animal. I understood her pain and defensiveness. The very first thought that came to me was "Oh Mighty God, when you grab that gal, she is going to do awesome things for You and Your Kingdom."

It was on that skiing trip, high on a snow-covered mountain, that Barb got more than she bargained for—she met Jesus.

Folks, as you read and participate in Barb's latest book, you will see the result of that "thought" that was planted 50+ years ago. God grabbed her attention, she accepted His invitation, and even though her life has not been perfect or issue-free she continues growing and serving our awesome God.

Luv you Barb and "you go girl!" Look out world! God ain't finished with His plan for your life.

—**Karyl Oules**
Former Ninth-Grade Youth Leader, Chelan, Washington

"Go out and stand before me on the mountain,"

*the L*ORD *told him. And as Elijah stood there,*

*the L*ORD *passed by, and a mighty*

windstorm hit the mountain.

It was such a terrible blast that the rocks

were torn loose,

*but the L*ORD *was not in the wind.*

After the wind there was an earthquake,

*but the L*ORD *was not in the earthquake.*

And after the earthquake there was a fire,

*but the L*ORD *was not in the fire.*

And after the fire there was the

sound of a gentle whisper."

1 Kings 19:11–12

LAZY AND FREE

When my author friend Joy DeKok invited me to contribute to her blog, I was both honored and flattered. You see, I have been in a self-imposed deep, dark writing cave for the past four years—hiding out from sharing my thoughts in print.

I'd become lazy and the *joy* of writing had been suppressed since a nasty departure from my church. I had been told, "Your services are no longer needed." I wasn't told why. They said they didn't need a reason. Gone were weekly and monthly deadlines. The only deadline in front of me now was having dinner on the table when my husband got home. (Deadlines I often missed.)

I had felt like the rug had been pulled out from under me. I was afraid to write—afraid that the anger, bitterness and hurt inside of me would surface in my writing. So I tucked my thoughts away, where no one except God and my closest friend could find them.

My life had changed. In a brief span I had lost my job, my church, my church friends, and my dad passed away. My mom was diagnosed with Parkinson's disease and we soon moved her into an assisted living community. I was still getting over the loss of my college roommate to pancreatic cancer and I lost my want or need to write.

When I drove the familiar path away from my job for the last time, it took two blocks for the light to come on. I felt something I didn't think I would feel. While I was hurt, I felt an overwhelming sense of peace and freedom.

God was so clearly saying to me, "No one can serve two masters. For you will hate one and love the other, or be devoted to one and despise the other. You cannot serve both God and money" (Luke 16:13). I had stayed at that job long past God calling me out and I knew it. I was working for the paycheck.

My Jesus had been telling me to go into the world, to share my story, His story. I was doing exactly that on weekends and feeling His incredible power working through me. It was something I did for the *joy* of serving Him, not for any financial rewards.

God kept speaking to me, giving me storylines to write and I ignored Him. I had a stack of notes of what He wanted me to share sitting on my desk, waiting. Not only was I being lazy, I was being disobedient to God's call on my life. Peter says in Acts 5:29, "We must obey God rather than human authority." My priorities had become to please man, get the work done and come back next week and do it all again. And truthfully, it was becoming rote. I also found that it is pointless to try to please man. Someone is always going to disagree or pick apart what you've done. Make a typo and someone is sure to point it out.

I was long overdue to leave, but kept hanging on. I could easily blame all the nasty things that happened on the enemy, but I refuse to give him any credit. I believe God made those last few years in that job unbearable, trying to move me out. And I stood firm. I was afraid of the future and afraid of not having a monthly paycheck, small as it was. I know full well that fear is not from the Lord, yet I hung in there.

I felt persecuted. No matter what I did, it was wrong. My vision for ministry and outreach was big and I realized I was in the wrong place for a person with a big vision. Persecuted, mocked, excluded, betrayed.

I was in good company. My Jesus experienced that too.

I've never shared my feeling about this publicly. I didn't want the bitterness to come through. But let me tell you this: I'm not bitter; I'm better! I am a new creation. "Therefore, if anyone is in Christ, he is a new creation; the old has gone, the new has come!" (2 Corinthians 5:17 NIV).

While I felt like I was in a deep dark valley, I remembered the words of Psalm 23:4: "Even when I walk through the dark valley of death, I will not be afraid, for you are close beside me. Your rod and your staff protect and comfort me." The Psalmist says we walk *through* the valley. The good news is we are not stuck there or abandoned! Eventually we come out on the other side! And He is there as we are on that journey. Always!

So if you have ever been told, "Your services are no longer needed," know this: God wants you in His service...forever. If you have ever been rejected, or simply feel you've been rejected, remember this: There is *Someone* who will never leave or forsake you. "Stay away from the love of money; be satisfied with what you have. For God has said, 'I will never fail you. I will never forsake you'" (Hebrews 13:5).

There were wonderful things that happened during this time that brought great *joy*. My son married a wonderful woman and two years later, they presented us with our first grandchild. Little Clara arrived almost two months early under extremely difficult circumstances. No longer was I surrounded by my friends from church for prayer support. I turned to my new church, but the people were, well...new. I shared my concerns anyway. God had me once again, right where He wanted me. And I turned to Him. My knees ached as I was on them constantly in prayer for our 2-pound, 15-ounce granddaughter. And He heard my prayers.

Had I still been trapped in that job, I would not have been able to spend as much time at the hospital as I did or tend to the daily needs of my mom and take her to doctors' appointments. My husband and I have been able to take off in the middle of the week and go to the beach, several times.

He is faithful to us and He expects us to be faithful and obedient to Him. We have one Master and His name is Jesus Christ.

When all else fails, when people walk away, remember this: God will not. "Be strong and courageous! Do not be afraid of them! The LORD your God will go ahead of you. He will neither fail you nor forsake you" (Deuteronomy 31:6).

Are you in that deep, dark cave hiding out? What is bogging you down, preventing you from being all that God has called you to do and be? Who or what has priority in your life? Have you lost your first love, Jesus Christ? He's waiting, right now, for your return. God will use your difficulties for His good, for His glory, if you let Him.

"So don't worry about having enough food or drink or clothing. Why be like the pagans who are so deeply concerned about these things? Your heavenly Father already knows all your needs, and he will give you all you need from day to day *if* you live for him and make the Kingdom of God your primary concern" (Matthew 6:31–33).

Join me on the journey. God will meet our needs when we put Him first! And oh has He!

✓ REALITY CHECK

Have you been wounded by the church? Have you put your faith in the people, instead of God? Remember the church is full of sinners, like you and me. While the church might abandon you, Jesus never will. You can take that to the bank.

⌛ PRAYER PAUSE

Heal my hurts, Lord. Turn my ashes into beauty. I am beyond thankful. Help me to model that beauty to those who still feel they are ashes. You can, You will, You did.

⬜ FOR THE RECORD

Two years after our precious and beautiful Clara was born, her equally precious and beautiful little sister Renee arrived. Yes, I am blessed.

For more information about Joy DeKok: www. joydekok.com

SITTING ON THE DOCK

"Sitting on the dock of the bay, watching time fade away." [1]

I was humming that old Otis Redding song as I sat on a dock over-looking Lake Crescent, a beautiful body of water west of Port Angeles, Washington, in the magnificent Olympic Mountain range. Even in late spring, the mountains were covered with snow. The beauty here is beyond description and reflecting its surroundings; the lake appears to be a brilliant teal color, yet so clear I can see the bottom of the lake from my perch on the dock.

Walking down to the lake, I noticed a sign posted on the boathouse, warning me that a cougar had been spotted in this area, followed by what to do if one approached you. It said, "Don't panic, don't run, face the cougar straight on, talk to it loudly and firmly and wave your arms." Panicking was not an option. (That would have been my *first* option and running my second.)

As I sat on the dock that afternoon, drinking in the beauty and the peacefulness of God's creation, I was thinking about the homework assignment I had just given the women attending the retreat where I was speaking.

The assignment: Find a psalm that addresses your needs at this particular moment in your life. I was thinking about what psalm I might select when it occurred to me that a cougar could easily sneak up behind me and attack. Would I even hear it? I was totally zoned out and zoned in on nature. I thought an option might be to go jump in the lake. I've been told to do that *many* times! A cougar is a cat, right? They hate the water. Then again, I hate freezing water, but I like living.

The thought no sooner entered my mind when right before my very eyes, a bald eagle flew directly in front of me, skimming the top of the water and landing on the other side of the inlet. I had my psalm! It was as if God had sent that eagle to tell me, "I have your back covered; fear not."

"Those who live in the shelter of the Most High will find rest in the shadow of the Almighty. This I declare of the LORD: He alone is my refuge, my place of safety; he is my God, and I am trusting him. For he will rescue you from every trap and protect you from the fatal plague. He will shield you with his wings. He will shelter you with his feathers. His faithful promises are your armor and protection. Do not be afraid of the terrors of the night, nor fear the dangers of the day" (Psalm 91:1–5). The psalm continues with "For he orders his angels to protect you wherever you go. They will hold you with their hands to keep you from striking your foot on a stone. You will trample down lions and poisonous snakes; you will crush fierce lions and serpents under your feet!" (91:11–13).

I watched with interest as the eagle began to flap his wings and dunk his head in the water. Smiling, I realized he was taking a bath. His big wings expanded, letting the air dry his feathers. I waited patiently and expectantly for the eagle to take off, wanting to take a picture of this magnificent bird. Finally, liftoff began and the eagle took off. I turned to grab my camera, but when I turned back, the eagle was gone. I had taken my eyes off of him for a second and he was gone.

And I realized something huge. I had turned to something worldly (my camera), to capture something a picture really wouldn't even do justice. I had taken my eyes off what God had sent, to capture what could only be held in my heart, in my mind, and in my soul.

Truth is, sometimes I do that with God too. I momentarily take my eyes off Him, and while He never leaves me, I sometimes feel I have left Him. We can hang pictures of Jesus in our homes and in our churches, but a picture truly does not capture who He is. We need Him captured in our heart, mind, and soul. We honestly don't even know if what the painter had in mind is what Jesus really looked like anyway, yet if you were to show someone a "picture" of Jesus, they would be able to immediately tell you who it was.

My Jesus reminded me. You don't need a picture of Me. You have Me in your heart. If you want to know what I look like, look within.

Jesus sent that eagle to take my mind off the danger of the cougar. He reminded me that He has my back. Nothing can touch me. I'm protected under His wings. He also reminded me that when I take my eyes off Him, I lose something.

"But those who wait on the LORD will find new strength. They will fly high on wings like eagles. They will run and not grow weary. They will walk and not faint" (Isaiah 40:31).

The rest of the day I sang, "And He will raise you up on eagles' wings, bear you on the breath of dawn. Make you to shine like the sun, and hold you in the palm of His hand." [2]

He's got you covered.

✓ REALITY CHECK

Keep your eyes on Jesus and you will find peace in the midst of danger. Look to the world for answers and you will quickly lose that peace. "Keep my eyes on you, Jesus, on whom my faith depends from start to finish" (Hebrews 12:2 paraphrased).

⏳ PRAYER PAUSE

Father, I realize that when I take my eyes off You, the world creeps in, blurring my vision—and my mind. Help me, Jesus, to focus on Your face. "...And the things of earth will grow strangely dim, in the light of His glory and grace." [3]

⬭ FOR THE RECORD

Each morning when I would awaken and look out the window, a deer would be in the field below. Several times throughout the day, I would come upon six deer grazing in one of the many open areas. On one occasion, I was standing in the middle of the herd, as close as ten feet from the lovely creatures. One of them looked up at me, as if to say, "Can I help you?" and then simply sat down.

While I was there to minister to women at a retreat, I found myself being ministered to in return by the beauty of what was around me.

✴ FOOTNOTES

1. Otis Redding and Steve Cropper
2. Michael Joncas
3. Helen H. Lemmel. "Turn Your Eyes upon Jesus." 1922. Public Domain

WHERE'S YOUR FOCUS?

Something wasn't right. My eyes were not focusing correctly on the road ahead as I drove down highway 101 along the coast of Oregon. I closed one eye, and then the other, and back to both together. My eyesight is a bit "off" anyway since I wear two different types of contacts lenses—one for distance and one for up close. (Yes, doubting Thomas, it does work, my brain *does* adjust.) It seems my *up close* contact was missing from my right eye, yet I knew I had put both contacts in my eyes that morning. Turning the car around, I went back to the vacation home where I was staying. Down on my hands and knees, with my nose to the floor, I searched the bathroom for my lost contact. Nothing!

Wouldn't you know it, this was one of the few times I didn't pack extra contacts. Here I was, out of town, miles from my optometrist, visualizing that unopened box of contacts lenses back home. Thankfully, I hadn't cleaned out my purse recently and I found my contact prescription receipt with the phone number of my optometrist on it. I called and got the prescription for my right eye and with numbers in hand, I drove to the local "all-everything store" and walked into the optical department. Yeah! They had the contact lens...but...she said she could not legally give it to me without the *written* prescription, *signed* by the doctor. There, just over the customer counter, within a reach and run, was the contact I needed, and couldn't have. The optical assistant called my clinic and asked them to FAX my prescription to her. I waited, and waited, and waited.

Finally, I told the woman that I had a luncheon meeting and just never mind. I'd wear my glasses. At lunch, I told the ladies what had happened and said, "Oh well, it's not like I don't have my glasses." I just said whatever and released it...or so I thought.

After lunch, I went back to the vacation home where I was staying and found the number to the optical department at the store I had just been in. Obviously, I had not been able to totally let go of my situation. I called the store to see if by any chance the FAX had come through. Yes, it had and off I went back downtown to get it.

Pulling out my credit card, I prepared to pay big bucks for the lens. The woman I had been so frustrated with earlier finally handed over the lens, legally. When I asked what I owed, she said there was no charge. Excuse me? No charge? Nope. Not a cent! This was a sample they had in, and they couldn't sell it. I vacillated between two thoughts...one, it was free, so why couldn't I have had it earlier? And secondly, gratitude. After all of this frustration, they had what I needed and it was free. Of course, thankfulness was not my first thought; it was irritation. I had basically had a mental meltdown, and after all the frustration, I heard the words, "no charge."

The day after the event, I went back to the house to unwind. In the bathroom, I started to take out my contacts and there in the sink, where I had looked several times, where I had run my hand around the sink, and run water down the drain, was my lost contact, hanging from the side of the sink. What? How? Unreal!

It was like the lens had dropped down out of nowhere, and oddly enough, it had not dried out and become brittle.

My heart did a God thump as I replayed the past day and a half.

I had been totally irritated with the lady in the optical department who would not give me the contact, and I was desperately trying not to let my inward thoughts show outwardly on my face or in my words. "Look lady, I'm a Christian speaker here on a mission from God to minister to the women in this town...now give me that!!" No, I didn't say that, but the thought ran through my head. I would have been a great ambassador for Christ had those thoughts come out of my mouth, don't you think?

Why did I have to go through this? Why wasn't my contact visible when I initially looked for it, not after I didn't care if I found it? Why the struggle? Why the frustration and irritation? Again, I had to be taught a lesson.

"No charge" echoed in my head. He orchestrated everything—at no charge! This was so like Him, with His free gift of salvation. Can't buy it, can't earn it, just have to accept it and say thank you. No charge.

Sometimes, we just have to say thanks and respond, with gratitude, joy and thankfulness in our hearts and in our actions. "God saved you by his special favor when you believed. And you can't take credit for this; it is a gift from God" (Ephesians 2:8).

In order to be all we can be for Him, we have to put off everything that hinders that relationship (like focusing on a contact lens). We also have to receive the free gift He offers, that free gift of salvation, of life with Him eternally. Just like the lady at the optical department who said, "no charge," Jesus says the same thing. No charge. Sins forgiven. Paid in full.

I lost a contact lens that day, and couldn't see. And by doing that, my eyes were opened to see even more clearly than before. More than that, my heart was open to see, to receive, and to go and share that "miracle for the day" with others.

An encounter with the living God cannot be kept secret. And I choose to believe it was Him, all the way, directing this entire scenario. He was waiting for me to go to Him first. "...And he will give you all you need from day to day if you live for him and make the Kingdom of

God your primary concern" (Matthew 6:33).

I hadn't done that. I'd put my needs above His. Oddly enough, this trip was all about the Kingdom of God, yet somewhere along the line, a molehill became a mountain and my focus turned inward.

Through this, I had become like the woman with the lost coin. She looked everywhere for it, sweeping the house (ouch) and looking everywhere until she found it. And when she did, she had to tell everyone (Luke 15:8–10). And that's how I felt. I went to church the next day with the woman in charge of the event where I'd spoken the day before. I had shared on Saturday my frustration with losing the contact lens... and now I was able to rejoice over that lost contact. But I couldn't rejoice until I'd release it to God with a *"whatever, it's not important, I can do without it"* attitude.

What was important was the mission He had sent me on, not my vain thoughts of how I looked with my glasses on. Looking back, I am ashamed of my thoughts—thoughts unbecoming an ambassador for Christ. The thoughts didn't come out through my mouth, but God knew what I was thinking. And that's bad enough because it's Him I represent, Him I want to please.

How good is your vision? Where is your focus—on the problem, or on the Provider? It matters not how you look, but Who you love.

✓ REALITY CHECK

Who are you when no one is watching?

Someone is, you know. God.

⌛ PRAYER PAUSE

Father, don't let my frustration lead to anger and my anger lead to sin. Help me to remember this: "Give all your worries and cares to God, for he cares about what happens to you" (1 Peter 5:7).

FOREVER IS...FOREVER!

Anticipating an upcoming event for a child seems like *forever*. The question is always, "When Mommy? When will it get here?" If the answer was "soon," the question was always, "when is soon?" A birthday, Christmas, the trip to Disneyland, last day of school...like I said...*forever*! Will the day ever arrive? Sometimes the anticipation just seems forever. While forever drags for a child, forever seems to come too quickly for us grown-ups.

Every third week of June, our town celebrates Planters' Day, in commemoration of the earthen dikes being built around the "bottomlands" to hold back the Columbia River, which allowed the farmers to plant their crops without fear of flooding. (No, I don't live in Holland, and no a little boy doesn't stick his finger in the dike to hold the waters back.)

Among the festivities in town during the celebration are a parade through the center of town, complete with the queen and her court, a frog-jumping contest, street dance, cake walk, traditional barbecue beef sandwiches, and a carnival. As a child it seems we waited forever for the carnival to come, and thanks to my grandma, my brother and sister and I had extra money to spend on the amusement park rides.

About the second week in June, we started nagging Mom. "Mommy, drive through the park! Please Mommy, please!" We wanted to see if the trucks carrying the amusement park rides had started to pull into town. Each day, we would drive through the park, and our excitement would build as the rides began to take shape. We would shout for joy "they're here, they're here!" when we saw our favorite rides being set up or grieve when we realized our favorite was missing that year. What a gyp!

My favorite childhood carnival ride was the octopus. I loved how the little car at the end of the long mechanical arm would spin around and around, up and down. Seems like the ride went on forever. One year, I braved the ride eight times in a row. Yahoo! What fun! My motto was "no guts, no glory!"

Today, many years later, I can barely watch the octopus operate. My head spins just to look at the ride in motion. Something I enjoyed so much as a child, and looked forward to forever, now gives me a splitting headache! Oh how times have changed.

Maybe this is all part of growing up. Could it be that forever word, maturity has finally hit? What gave me a thrill at age 10 or even 20 doesn't seem to give me the same thrill at 50, or 60. Wait! Yes it does! I still love Planters' Day. I still see it through childlike eyes. I still get the little heart leap when I see the trucks in the park (and yes I drive through every day watching the progress). Growing up, however, does not have to mean growing old. Maturing does not have to mean getting stuffy or forgetting what our first love was like. While we need to put away our childish things, we need to remember what it was like to be childlike. To remember the thrill, the excitement, the anticipation of what was coming.

Remember when you first discovered who Jesus was? Go back to that time. Did you sing about how Jesus loves you because the Bible tells you so? If I could have one line, as a statement of faith, that summarizes my beliefs, it would be this: "Jesus loves me, this I know, for the Bible tells me so." Do you think that is childlike for me to say that? Great! Cause I am a child—of God. "See how very much our heavenly Father loves us, for he allows us to be called his children, and we really are!" (1 John 3:1).

We are His children right now...whatever our earthly age. But just as our body grows and matures, so should our love and knowledge of our Father.

"When I was a child, I spoke like a child and thought and reasoned as a child does. But when I grew up, I put away childish things" (1 Corinthians 13:11).

Sometimes as adults, it seems to me that we complicate this whole religion thing. We become more concerned about rules and structure than we do about a relationship with Jesus and praise and worship to Him. We become self-sufficient, instead of relying on His sufficiency. We grow independent, instead of remaining dependent on Him. We lose sight of Whose we are, forever.

What have you been looking forward to *forever*? What have you been anticipating *forever*? Are you as excited about those things as you are about knowing one day you will be with Jesus forever? How are you preparing for *forever*?

"*Forever* God is faithful, *forever* God is strong, *forever* God is with us, *forever and ever.*" [1]

Hold on tight to that.

✓ REALITY CHECK

How are you preparing for *forever*? Are you growing closer to Him and developing an intimate relationship with Him?

⧖ PRAYER PAUSE

Father, help me to have a childlike faith that trusts and worships You with total abandon. Help me to grow in my faith, my trust and my love for You.

⬚ FOR THE RECORD

Jesus welcomed little children into His presence. Mark 10:13–16 tells us about parents who brought their children to see Jesus, but evidently the disciples thought only big people were welcomed, that children would be a bother. Jesus, displeased by what He saw happening, said, "'Let the children come to me. Don't stop them! For the Kingdom of God belongs to such as these. I assure you, anyone who doesn't have their kind of faith will never get into the Kingdom of God.' Then he took the children in his arms and placed his hands on their heads and blessed them."

✱ FOOTNOTES

1. © Chris Tomlin © Copyright 2001 worshiptogether.com Songs (ASCAP)/ sixsteps Music (ASCAP) (both admin. by EMI CMG Publishing)

WEIGHTY CHALLENGES

Taking the weight off was the easy part. Keeping it off has been, to put it mildly, a challenge.

While on my weight-loss program, I was required to check in at the center 20 miles away, three times a week to weigh in, and meet with a counselor. We celebrated each week as we watched the digital number on the scales go down, and I was encouraged not to worry if I had gained .06 pounds. (What, me worry?)

Each day, I knew exactly how much of each food group I could eat, and each day, I faithfully weighed, measured, and logged in my food journal what I had consumed.

The accountability of checking in was a necessary part of my success story. The visual effect of filling in those little boxes in my journal gave me a weird sense of accomplishment. I graphed my weight loss and watched the dots connect in a downward path toward my goal. The day I reached that goal, everyone at the center (and probably everyone at the mall) knew it, as I let out a big whoop and holler.

While on this program, my eating choices were limited, especially the first week. Weighing and measuring food became a habit, not a chore. Without doing this, I found I was actually depriving myself of the amount of food allowed.

Structure was the name of my game while on this program. Now I believe in structure, but I also believe in spontaneity *within* structure. Forget it! Spontaneity didn't occur until the stabilization and maintenance plan. I did not "cheat" once.

It's that spontaneity that gets me in trouble. Being on maintenance, the sky is the limit—within reason. Maintenance lasts a year, and the accountability check-in is down to once a week, instead of three times. I've moved past writing down what I eat and weighing the foods. I see a scone, I eat it. I drive by a Starbucks, I stop (love those caramel lattés). There are too many choices to make, and some days, I don't make the right ones. Getting on the bathroom scales reinforces my bad decisions.

When I made a commitment to follow Christ while in high school, I made the right choice, for a while. I went to youth group, attended church, and read my Bible. I was excited about my faith. I had an accountability group of friends and youth leaders to keep me on track. Being with people who shared my beliefs made it easier to stay on course.

Then, I left home and the choices were more difficult. Suddenly, my world expanded. No longer was I on a structured program with accountability, but more like maintenance, with more choices being tossed at me than I knew what to do with. It was my choice to make bad decisions or not; my choice not to seek a church or fellowship group. My choice, my decision, and they weren't always good decisions. And one bad decision, one piece of chocolate leads to another... and another...and another.

Romans 12:2 says, "Don't copy the behavior and customs of this world, but let God transform you into a new person by changing the way you think." What was off-limits for me as a new Christian became exciting and I wanted to experience all the world had to offer. I thought *this* was living life to the fullest. I had flung that narrow gate wide open and scripture tells us that "the highway to hell is broad and its gate is wide" (Matthew 7:13). In other words, the road that leads to destruction is wide. I was traveling that road.

I did better with my eating when I had narrow, limited choices and accountability. No cheating or I'd be found out. And I do better in my Christian life when I have someone who holds me accountable. No cheating, as I get found out (and God knows anyway).

On the outside, it's evident that I've changed. New body, new hairdo, but what about a new attitude? Philippians 2:5 tells us, "Your attitude should be the same that Christ Jesus had." We can choose that attitude or not. The choice is always ours. We can choose to love as Christ loves, to be humble, to be a servant to all, and to look for ways to serve people. First Corinthians 2:16 says that "we have the mind of Christ." Wow! I have the mind of Christ? On what day?

Joshua said to the people of Israel, "Choose today whom you will serve...as for me and my family, we will serve the LORD" (Joshua 24:15).

Joshua was determined to serve the LORD. Are we? Do our choices reflect that decision? Are we able to live in this world and not get sucked up into what the world considers acceptable behavior? Romans 12:2 tells us not to get sucked up in what the world says is okay. (Or should I say what the world says is PC...Politically Correct?)

I would encourage you to put off your former self; to put on Christ. I'm talking seriously here...put on Christ! Get someone to hold you accountable. Do you go to church? Great! Do you put into practice what is preached, or walk away unchanged?

"For if you just listen and don't obey, it is like looking at your face in a mirror but doing nothing to improve your appearance. You see yourself, walk away, and forget what you look like" (James 1:23–24).

✓ REALITY CHECK

Check-in or check-out. The choice is yours. Make the right decision. Find someone to get in your face and hold you accountable.

⧗ PRAYER PAUSE

Jesus, help me to stay on the path that leads to You. Your Word says, "Enter through the narrow gate. For wide is the gate and broad is the road that leads to destruction, and many enter through it. But small is the gate and narrow the road that leads to life, and only a few find it" (Matthew 7:13–14 NIV).

Father, don't let the world cut me off, tailgate or run me off the road. Help me to keep my eyes on the road ahead—on You.

⧉ FOR THE RECORD

I've gained the weight back and the weight-loss clinic has gone out of business. But the Word of the Lord stands forever.

STUMBLING ALONG

"**W**hat part of 'you are hurt' don't you understand?" Those words were spoken directly to me, in my face, loudly, and with hands waving, by my new nurse practitioner.

Gulp! "But, but, but, but," I said. "You don't understand."

"No buts!" she said forcefully. "Stop and I mean *stop* using that wrist! If you were 13, I'd put you in a cast, instead of a brace. Now stop using it, or I will!"

I knew I had met my match. I tried to explain that I am a "doer," a Martha personality, who can't sit still and has to be doing stuff. Even that didn't set well with this bossy woman, as she began a dissertation on the pros and cons of Mary and Martha.

"You go girl!" I said, smiling. "How do you know about Mary and Martha?" Come to find out, she had done a Bible study on them. This medical professional, who I had just met, was a Christian. I didn't consider she might *not* know who Martha was when I started name dropping. It was as easy as, "I'm a Martha" to begin a conversation about church.

But did I take her advice of "do not use that wrist"? I think those of you who know me know the answer to that one. And so, my wrist still hurts.

It was one of those klutz moments where the curb jumped up and tripped me. One of those moments of going down on all fours and coming up with bloody knees, elbows and oh yes, a hurt wrist from trying to catch myself with my left arm.

For most people, a wounded left wing might not slow them down. But I'm not like most people—I'm left-handed. And so the challenges began, and my wrist continued to hurt.

Challenges presented themselves, like eating and cooking. Using my right wrist and arm to pick up a frying pan was awkward. I could not open a jar since I had no strength to hold the jar in my left hand and open it with my right. Oh I learned to adapt, using the crook in my elbow as a vise-grip. But adapting made doing chores slower—and remember, I'm a fast-moving Martha. And so, the wrist continues to hurt.

"What part of 'no' don't you understand?" God asked Adam and Eve in the third chapter of Genesis. Okay, He didn't really put it that way, but you know He had to be thinking it. They were told they could eat from any tree in the Garden, except one. And they ate from it anyway. You couldn't follow just one rule? And God began to hurt.

"Don't look back," Mrs. Lot was told as her family hurried out of Sodom and Gomorrah. God told her one thing: "Don't look back." She ignored Him, looking back to see what she was leaving and became a statue of salt. (Read Genesis 19.) When it rains, it pours. And God continued to hurt.

Ananias and Sapphira sold property and gave the money to the church. Good for them! Problem was, they lied about it. While giving to the church was a good thing, saying all the proceeds from the sale were donated (when they kept some for themselves) was not a good thing. Due to their lack of honesty and deception, both were struck dead. And God continued to hurt.

Every time we are faced with "what part of 'don't do it' do you not understand?" and do it anyway, we sin and we suffer. And we don't suffer alone. God suffers with us. And God continues to hurt.

Our goal is to keep our focus on God, so the bumps in life, the distractions of the world that pull our focus off of the godly and onto the worldly, won't trip us up.

Romans 9:32 says, "They stumbled over the great rock in their path." That rock was Jesus and we stumble over Him too, when we pit the immoral vs. the moral issues—when we take our eyes off Him. We stumble when we look to the world for adventure, support, affirmation, and validity. We stumble when we think we know best, when we go it on our own and leave Jesus behind. And we stumble when we don't ask for help. The light of Jesus always exposes the darkness.

I had stumbled over that great rock (the curb) that day because I wasn't watching where I was going. My mind was on where I needed to be and what I needed to get done. My arms were full of stuff, totally loaded down, and I stubbornly thought I could carry one more thing down the stairs to the church rummage sale, instead of making two or three or even four trips. And I fell. And my wrist began to hurt, and God hurt with me.

Sin was introduced into the world by one simple act...want of what someone couldn't have. The "I know better than God" mentality was introduced. And God is hurt by this attitude.

With all the freedom to choose that we have—the freedom *to do*—what part of *do not*, do we *not* understand?

"Mark out a straight path for your feet. Then those who follow you, though they are weak and lame, will not stumble and fall but will become strong" (Hebrews 12:13). We are to be examples to the world and as examples, not cause others to stumble.

Jude 1:24 wraps it up this way: "And now, all glory to God, who is able to keep you from stumbling..." *He* is able to keep you from stumbling. But you have to watch where you are going, focusing on the Father.

And now, God is smiling. (And I need to go put ice on my wrist.)

✓ REALITY CHECK

Are you tripping over your own feet, your life circumstances, and your want to do things your own way? Look up!

⧗ PRAYER PAUSE

Father, help me to stop looking at what I want to accomplish and focus on what You want to accomplish through me. I'm sorry for the hurt I have caused You through my thoughtless actions. Thank You for Your forgiveness.

WALK FREE

Standing in church one Sunday morning, the words to a song we were singing penetrated my heart. My eyes filled with tears, blurring my vision. I found it difficult to see, let alone sing due to the huge lump in my throat.

The words: "You took my sin and my shame; You took my sickness and healed all my pain. Thank You Lord."[1]

My heart was drawn to, and convicted of, my sinful nature and my need to confess my sins daily to my Jesus. And the added reminder was not to dwell on the sin because through Jesus Christ, my sins have been forgiven. Oh yes, and to say thank you!

I'd like to tell you I'm not still sinning. I'd like to tell you that once I've confessed and received that gift of forgiveness that I'm free from *all* sin. I'd like to be able to say, "I won't do it again." But I'd be lying.

We all have this sinful nature built into us. We sin. We ask for forgiveness. We receive the forgiveness, and oops, there we go again. Second verse, same as the first.

First John 1:8–10 says, "If we say we have no sin, we are only fooling ourselves and refusing to accept the truth. But if we confess our sins to him, he is faithful and just to forgive us and to cleanse us from every wrong. If we claim we have not sinned, we are calling God a liar and

26

showing that his word has no place in our heart."

Yikes! I certainly do not want to be accused of calling God a liar. Paul tells us in Romans 3:23, "For all have sinned; all fall short of God's glorious standard." All sin. All fall.

The beautiful promise that follows is this: "Yet now God in his gracious kindness declares us not guilty. He has done this through Christ Jesus, who has freed us by taking away our sins" (Romans 3:24). Did you see that? Not guilty!

Since God has declared us not guilty and freed us from the sins of our past, why do we hang on to our sins like He hasn't? God is the judge. He alone holds the gavel and He's banging it down saying, you are innocent...you are released...you are free!

God spoke to me through this song, assuring me that the sins of the past, and the shame that followed them, are gone—forgiven and forgotten. Wiped clean. Never happened. Gone, no more.

Thank You, Lord! Thank You, Lord!

Christ has opened the prison doors we find ourselves behind. Take that get-out-of-jail-free card and move on! And when you step out into the fresh air of freedom, remember this: "So Christ has really set us free. Now make sure that you stay free, and don't get tied up again in slavery to the law" (Galatians 5:1).

We don't like to admit that we are sinners, I mean *really* admit it. Not to ourselves, or to anyone else. Yet God knows. He looks into our heart, our mind and sees right through our deception.

The song continues with action required on our part: "With an outstretched arm I will bless Your name." [1]

I will indeed bless His name and show my love for Him with my arms outstretched. That's how He showed his love for me...with outstretched arms.

"But Christ has rescued us from the curse pronounced by the law.

When he hung on the cross, he took upon himself the curse for our wrongdoing" (Galatians 3:13).

He forgives our every wrong, every time.

✓ REALITY CHECK

You sin. I sin. We all sin. We confess and ask for forgiveness and wham...we sin again. Yet God's grace and love continues to forgive us...again and again and again.

⧗ PRAYER PAUSE

Jesus, Name above all names, thank You for Your grace that covers my sins—past, present, and future. Help me to learn from my past mistakes and grow in my relationship with You.

✸ FOOTNOTES

1. © Don Moen and Paul Baloche. 2004 Integrity's Hosanna! Music

DECIDING TO CHOOSE

I'm having a tough time making a decision today. It's well past noon, the sun is shining, and I'm sitting in a big red swivel chair, gazing out on the choppy waters of Hood Canal, near the Olympic Mountains in Washington State. The seagulls are flying low overhead (look out!) and the ducks are bobbing up and down on the water. A couple of days ago, I was in awe as a two whales swam by. Oh yeah, and there's an annoying bird pecking for bugs just outside the window.

Usually making a decision like this is not difficult, but today, I'm struggling. The decision is: Should I, or should I not, get dressed? I know, it seems like a minor decision, but right now, even the minors have become majors. I can't choose: Dressed or not dressed? No one is going to see me. There is no one here to care if I'm not wearing makeup, clean clothes...or deodorant for that matter. I'm here alone for the week and I haven't talked with anyone in days. I have no reason to. I wonder if my vocal cords still function.

I'm on my yearly battery recharge or "I want to be alone" week, trying to catch up on sleep, reading, and my relationship with my Jesus. I've been having trouble hearing Him through the clanging distractions of life.

God has sent the sun, with blue skies during the day, and the wind and rain at night. Calm vs. storm. It's perfect! It's like life. Good days, bad days, in-between days. The weather does not concern me. I'm safe and warm inside the house. The windows give me the only view to the world that I need. And the view is spectacular.

This has been a busy year. Speaking every weekend during the spring and working on editing my second book during the summer and fall. Too many choices and too many decisions to make. Friction to the left, controversy to the right, and finding myself smack dab in the middle. Health of family, friends and some personal health oddities have sent me to my knees more that I can tell you. In the middle of this, my husband decided to retire from his job, no warning—just, "I'm done!" That created a whole new set of challenges, for *both* of us.

Deuteronomy 30:20 talks about making an important decision. It says, "Choose to love the LORD your God and to obey him and commit yourself to him, for he is your life." It certainly makes my getting dressed decision seem rather insignificant.

Choices. Decisions. We even have the choice to reject God. He doesn't make us love him. We have the freedom to choose. However, we are told in Deuteronomy 6:5, "And you must love the LORD your God with all your heart, all your soul, and all your strength." Did you read that? *Must* love.

Following and obeying God is a conscious choice, a decision of our will. Joshua told the children of Israel to choose, right now, who you are going to follow, to serve. And then went on to say that he and his household were going to serve the LORD (paraphrase of Joshua 24:15).

It all goes back to choices. We all make thousands of them in one day, big and little. Don't forget to include God in those decisions. Line them up with what He wants for you. Even if they are as simple as "should I get dressed?"

✓ **REALITY CHECK**

Do you take time alone to be with God? Maybe you need to put yourself in a "timeout," even if only for five minutes in the bathroom. Your choice!

⧗ **PRAYER PAUSE**

Father, help me at the beginning of each day to make a conscious decision to follow Your lead. Let Your will be done! When life throws me a curve ball, help me to step out of the way and let it pass. And when my head hits the pillow at night, help me to rest in You.

DAMAGED GOODS

It was a rare day for me, a day I'd called in sick to work. It wasn't so odd that I was ill, but that I'd *reported out* from work. I never call in sick. Never! So you know just how under the weather I was.

The phone rang, waking me from my nap. The woman at the other end of the line told me my son Matt had been injured while on his kindergarten class field trip. (This was before the days of a cell phone in every pocket, and she was calling from a Good Samaritan's house nearby.)

Sick or not, this mother threw on clothes and headed to the park 20 miles away—no makeup and hair stuck to my head. I found Matt, sitting with his teacher on a picnic table bench, her arms holding him close.

Gathering him up, I drove across town to the medical clinic. Several hours later, we emerged from the clinic...Matt with a cast on his left arm. A thrill ride down the park slide had resulted in a broken arm.

In the car on the way home, the words that came out of this six-year-old's quivering mouth were, "I'm broken." He thought he was damaged goods.

Fast forward a few years and once again, I get the call that my son is sick. Off this mom goes, rushing down the freeway to be with him. Out of nowhere, the rubber base of a construction cone was flying at me. With no place to go, I took the hit...and lost the right side mirror of my car.

I kept driving, with the mirror hanging from the side of my pretty blue car. My *brand-new car*, was now broken...damaged goods. What it took to make it good as new was the dealer putting on a brand-new mirror. My broken car went from damaged goods to good as new.

Soon after that, a trip through the car wash resulted in a chipped windshield and deep scratches along the driver's side door. An antenna that had been magnetically attached to the truck ahead of me in the carwash had detached during the wash and wrapped around the spongy washing arms. As the brushes began to move along my car, so did the antenna—back and forth on my car. Wham! Slam! Scratch! Crash! I had no place to go—no escape.

When the arms of the washing machine finally pulled back in mid-wash, I stepped on the gas and jetted out of the carwash, suds and all. The chip was small, but it was in my line of vision and I knew if I didn't attend to it, the chip would only get bigger, eventually growing to a cracked line across the windshield. The chip wasn't obvious to anyone but me, unless you were really looking closely. My still-new car, was once again broken...damaged goods.

I tried to repair the scratches. Rubbing compound would not remove the marks as they were too deep. It took a professional at the body shop to fill them in with putty, sand it down, and repaint. Broken, damaged goods, now good as new.

In all three cases, something was damaged or broken. In all three cases, they were made new, made whole. The broken arm healed; the car looked like new again, after both repairs. But had the problems not been fixed, they would have gotten worse. Matt's arm might have healed crooked, causing weakness. The mirror was a safety issue, plus it could have fallen off, creating a problem for someone else driving behind me. And the windshield chip could have spread to a full-blown crack, working its way across the entire windshield. The scratches could have begun to rust.

Something *minor* can always become something *major* if we don't take care of it.

Jesus dealt with broken people throughout the Bible. A Jesus encounter caused their brokenness to be healed. Jesus said, "Healthy people don't need a doctor—sick people do." (Read Matthew 9:12.)

Jesus took people who were living with broken lives, who in the world's eyes were damaged goods, and He made them whole. Some of those people the Bible refers to are the woman at the well, the woman caught in adultery, and the sinful woman. All broken, all damaged goods. All made good as new after an encounter with Jesus.

God took an Old Testament woman, identified as a prostitute, and used her as part of His plan. This woman, Rahab, is listed in what Hebrews 11 calls the "great hall of faith." A prostitute and an ancestor of Jesus, Rahab is remembered for her faith, not her occupation. (Read her story in Joshua 2 and 6.)

God said David was a man after his own heart, yet David fell short more times than we can count. Broken, damaged goods, restored by God.

You see, repentance opens the way to forgiveness and restoration. No matter how low we sink, how broken we are or how damaged we become, God is willing to buy us back. He did this through the sacrifice of His Son, Jesus Christ. Our sins, past, present, and future were nailed to the cross with Jesus. Gone!

First Peter 2:24 says, "He personally carried away our sins in his own body on the cross so we can be dead to sin and live for what is right. You have been healed by his wounds."

Our damaged goods have been made good as new.

God doesn't promise that we won't be damaged in life. But He does promise He will be with us. Psalm 91 tells us that He will rescue and protect us. He tells us not to fear the terror of the night, that no evil will conquer us and no plague will come near us. He sends His angels to protect us, holding us in their hands. He says he will rescue those who love him. Call on Him and He will answer. (My paraphrase.)

In God's eyes, we are no longer broken or damaged people. Confes-sion, repentance, and zowee! He has made us whole! God's grace covers it all. Second Corinthians 3:4–5 reassures us with: "Such confidence as this is ours through Christ before God. Not that we are competent in ourselves to claim anything for ourselves, but our competence come from God" (NIV).

The broken places, damaged parts, of our lives are gone. He has removed them. If we keep recalling them, perhaps we don't really feel God has forgiven or healed us.

Like Matt's teacher who held him in her arms, comforting him, God holds us in the palm of His hands. Go there and rest in Him.

✓ REALITY CHECK

If you have asked for forgiveness from God for your sins, and reminders of them keep popping in your head, it's not God's voice you are hearing. It's the enemy's. You have been forgiven "as far away from us as the east is from the west" (Psalm 103:12).

⧖ PRAYER PAUSE

Thank You, Jesus, for Your love and forgiveness. You don't see me as damaged good; You see me as whole, as Your beloved child. It's Your love that keeps me going.

THE BABY HAS ARRIVED

After months of preparation, I've finally held my new little bundle of joy in my hands. My second book has been delivered.

I am amazed that I went through this birthing process again. Book one had enough labor pains; you'd have thought I'd learned my lesson. But no, just like having a baby, you forget the pain you experienced at delivery, once you hold that precious bundle in your arms...and you actually think you might want to do it again. Okay, so not right away!

My babies, or books, were delivered five years apart. Enough time to only have one in diapers at a time, dontcha think? Enough time to forget the pain of the first labor. You would think the second delivery would have gone smoother as I now knew what to expect.

Book one was birthed to an inexperienced mother. I had many decisions to make along the way, all of which were foreign to this first-time mother, I mean author. I didn't know the ins and outs of publishing. All terms were Greek to me. I depended on the guidance of my birthing coach, aka, project manager. The artistic and avid book reader side of me knew exactly how I wanted this book to look. I had the cover designed to my specifications, right down to the last detail. The drawing was the perfect caricature of me.

I certainly never expected a speaking ministry to follow the book release. I had several conversations with God about this. "I can't, I can't, I can't," was my battle cry. "Please don't make me do this!" And He would say, "No you can't, but I can. Go, go, go!"

Jesus said to "Go into all the world and preach the Good News to everyone, everywhere" (Mark 16:15). I certainly didn't feel I had the skills to speak. Yet I knew who did, and who went with me. Again and again I have said, "God doesn't call the qualified; He qualifies the called."

And so I went. At the majority of events, I was welcomed with open arms. At one, I wanted to scream. While the ladies seemed to embrace me, the woman in charge sneered at me every time I walked by. It was hard not to take it personally. I felt rejected, even though she was the only one out of the 60 ladies present who snubbed me.

I'm trying hard to realize that everyone isn't going to like me. Our personalities don't always mesh with those who are opposites, or those who are like us for that matter. There will always be naysayers, who seem to have a louder voice than "yeah-sayers." We can be oil, we can be vinegar. We can be like Mutt and Jeff, or Oscar and Felix. Sometimes the combinations don't always blend.

The disciples of Jesus were told to shake the dust off their feet. "If a village doesn't welcome you or listen to you, shake off the dust of that place from your feet as you leave" (Matthew 10:14). Oh, if it were really that easy! Did they really not want to be loved and accepted everywhere they went?

Now my second baby is here. With that, more responsibility. More choices. More decisions. I've come to the conclusion I hate choices and making decisions. Why can't life be strictly vanilla and chocolate? Do we have to add sprinkles?

I thought the birthing process would be easier the second time around, but it was in fact harder. I thought I knew what to expect. What I learned from the first baby didn't apply to the second. It was a whole new process. I'd become more picky, the publisher was more picky (or at least in my mind he was). I had no project manager to guide me, but a wonderful picky editor who gently (or not) showed me the way. She wanted it done right, not only because that was her job, but because she was a friend.

In Matthew 13:55, the people are looking at Jesus and saying, "He's *just* a carpenter's son..." (italics mine). Jesus was rejected in His own hometown. The people had watched Him play in the sandbox and grow into adulthood. And now, they couldn't believe that this hometown boy was performing miracles. They were unable to separate the boy they knew as a child from the man He had become. They couldn't look past the "we knew you when you were a snot-nosed kid" to the message He brought to them now.

"Can anything good come out of Nazareth?" asked Nathaniel in John 1:46. He was in disbelief. From a distance, he had this preconceived idea of who this man was, which was shattered once he met Jesus.

Sometimes that happens with us too. We have preconceived ideas of how people should act. We put people in a box and tell them to stay there. Risk-takers for God don't do well in boxes.

But something good can come from anyplace, once Jesus takes over. The "becoming" process takes time. It takes putting off your old self, and allowing Jesus to turn you into a new creation. Second Corinthians 5:17 says, "Those who become Christians become new persons. They are not the same anymore, for the old life is gone. A new life has begun!" I love that verse. For me, it hits the proverbial nail right on my stubborn head.

With this new life, Paul tells us, "We try to live in such a way that no one will be hindered from finding the Lord by the way we act, and so no one can find fault with our ministry. In everything we do we try to show that we are true ministers of God. We patiently endure troubles and hardships and calamities of every kind. We have been beaten, been put in jail, faced angry mobs, worked to exhaustion, endured sleepless nights, and gone without food" (2 Corinthians 6:3–5). Been there, done that. Tried that, fallen short, and picked myself up and continued on.

In the face of rejection, Paul said, "We serve God whether people honor us or despise us, whether they slander us or praise us" (2 Corinthians 6:8). He knew not to let people's opinion of him control his service to God. Oh how I wish I was there!

✓ REALITY CHECK

If God calls you, He will equip you. "When" He calls, go! God will use you in ways you never imagined.

⧖ PRAYER PAUSE

God, my prayer is that You would help me to get out of the way, so You can have Your way in me. Empty me of my will and fill it with Yours.

I WANT IN!

Reading the headlines in today's paper caused my spirit to soar. The caption read: "Players Report for Spring Training." Whooohoooo. Baseball season is upon us. In a few short weeks, I'll be hearing those words that are music to my ears, "Let's Play Ball!"

Oh I know the *real* games won't start for a month or so, that spring training is just that—training. It's about getting back in shape, reconnecting with old and new teammates and learning how to play as a team again. I'm excited just anticipating the start of the season. The winter blahs are behind me...the new season is about to begin.

In baseball, there are nine players in the game for each team. Many of those are the *everyday* players. Yet even those players have backups, those who can go into the game at any given moment. That is especially true with the pitchers. You have the starter, the short reliever, the set-up man, and the closer. Then you have the left-handed pitcher and the right-handed pitcher, so you can play the odds, the percentages. Right-handed batters don't usually hit well off right-handed pitchers. Same with lefties against lefties. There are pitchers who excel at the fastball, the slider, the sinker, the splitter, the curve, and oh yes, the knuckleball.

During the off-season (those months of my winter blahs), the team management is busy making player trades with other teams. The roster of players from last year most likely won't be the same as this year. The new pitcher we booed while on another team the previous year is now ours to cheer. We are a fickle bunch, for sure, but that's the loyalty of the fans. We root for our own—even if he was on another team last year. Change the logo on your hat to ours, and we love you.

Now if you aren't a baseball fan, what I just said probably didn't make a bit of sense. But it's crystal clear to me, and I'm getting pumped just writing the words.

Jesus had His own team. We call them disciples. He started with 12 on His team—Simon (Peter), James, John, Andrew, Philip, Bartholomew, Matthew, Thomas, James, Thaddeus, Simon the Zealot, and Judas Iscariot These men were drafted to be on the expansion team. The New Testament is filled with names of people who played on Jesus' team. Many didn't get recognition. They just did what was asked of them, day after day, filling in where needed.

Mid-season, someone had to be called up from the minor leagues (Matthias), as one of the players (Judas) left the team. The original team was in training for three years, walking with Jesus, getting into shape, and learning the rules of the game. Jesus was preparing them to play the game without Him. Sometimes they questioned the rules, sometimes they wanted to change them, one bet against him with a betrayal.

When Jesus went to the cross, His followers were in a state of shock. Was this the end of the season? They huddled together, wondering what to do next. What would they do without their main man—the guy who was their manager, ace pitcher, and homerun hitter?

On Palm Sunday, Jesus made His World Series ticker-tape parade entrance through Jerusalem on His donkey motorcade. Fans came out in droves to cheer Him as He passed through town. Confetti was dropped from tall buildings—I mean the people waved palm leaves. By the end of the week, the fans turned fickle; the cheering was over, and the jeering began. Their favorite player, who was loved or hated, had been dropped. The wood He carried on His way to Calvary was not a Louisville Slugger bat made of crafted ash, but a cross, made of rough common wood.

It was over. Jesus was crucified, died, and was buried. The winning team was now the cellar dweller. The momentum has ceased, or so they thought. The *great baseball philosopher* Yogi Berra said, "It ain't over 'til it's over." And it wasn't.

Those first fans to the tomb that Easter morning (women by the way) heard the words they had longed to hear: "He isn't here! He has been raised from the dead, just as he said would happen" (Matthew 28:6).

Just like followers of baseball long to hear, "let's play ball," the followers of Jesus were awestruck when they heard, "He is risen!" The game wasn't over. It was just beginning.

The work for those first followers of Jesus was about to begin. They were prepared. They'd been under the tutelage of the Coach.

✓ REALITY CHECK

Whose team are you on? Team Jesus or Team Politically Correct? Which rules do you follow? Rules the Bible has given us, or rules the world throws at us?

⧗ PRAYER PAUSE

Jesus, my heart's desire is to play on Your team, every day. I don't want to be a bench warmer or the batboy, or the locker room attendant. My goal is to play an active position on the playing field You have given me, to the best of my ability, with Your help and guidance.

WHAT'S IN YOUR LUGGAGE?

"We are marching to Camp Evergreen, Camp Evergreen!" Oh how I loved that one week every summer when I would attend Girl Scout Camp. I was packed a month ahead of time, living out of the open suit-case in my bedroom, wanting to make sure no items were skipped on the list of things to bring to camp. If I used an article of clothing from the suitcase, I repacked when the laundry was done, rather than put-ting it in my dresser. It was easy to pack for a week with a list that said "bring only what is listed." This was *way* before we even considered the forbidden items of tobacco, alcohol, firearms, or "transistor" radios (not to mention cell phones). Candy might have been the only contraband anyone tried to sneak in.

Fifty years later, I wish someone would give me a list of items to pack. On weekends when I am out of town speaking at a retreat, I struggle with exactly what to take to wear. Will the weather be nice or will it rain? (Travel within Oregon and Washington, I *know* the answer to that question.) Will the retreat center have trails to hike? Will my room be warm? Will I need a coat, a sweater, hiking boots or my flannel nightgown? Are towels and linens provided?

Next question...how dressy is the event? I search my closet looking for clothes to wear and pull out half a dozen or so pieces that "might work." Then I hang the clothes on the closet door and look them over for a couple of days, trying to narrow down what I might feel like wearing. Basic black, brown, gray or blue? I can't take them all. (Well I could if I were driving, but traveling by airplane limits my wardrobe.)

How much free time will there be at the event? Should I take a book? Which one? What will I feel like reading? I end up packing six and not reading any of them.

Too many choices. Too many decisions. Too many distractions. I find myself more concerned about what I will wear, than what I will share.

Jesus addresses my dilemma in Matthew 6:28: "And why worry about your clothes? Look at the lilies and how they grow. They don't work or make their clothing."

And He gets me where I pack with this: "When I sent you out and told you to travel light, to take only the bare necessities, did you get along all right?"

"Certainly," they said, "we got along just fine" (Luke 22:35 MSG).

If the disciples were told to pack light, why can't I? Why am I so concerned about wearing the right clothes? Truth is, I'd rather be in jeans, a T-shirt, and barefoot.

Peter tells us: "Don't be concerned about the outward beauty that depends on fancy hairstyles, expensive jewelry, or beautiful clothes. You should be known for the beauty that comes from within, the unfading beauty of a gentle and quiet spirit, which is so precious to God (1 Peter 3:3–4).

The Message puts it this way: "What matters is not your outer appearance—the styling of your hair, the jewelry you wear, the cut of your clothes—but your inner disposition. Cultivate inner beauty, the gentle, gracious kind that God delights in."

People can't see what is on the inside unless you let it shine—through your words, your actions, your face, your life. Have you ever had anyone say, "It's written all over your face"? Boy, I have! I don't have a poker face, for sure. What I'm thinking and feeling usually is reflected on my face and in my actions. Some days, I just pack better than others. Some days, I need to unpack the dirty laundry and replace it with clean clothes.

What I need is a list—a list of things to pack each day, like I did at camp.

Colossians 3:12 provides that list, just like Camp Evergreen provided the list. Here it is: "Since God chose you to be the holy people whom he loves, you must clothe yourselves with tenderhearted mercy, kindness, humility, gentleness, and patience."

With all of those things packed, He tells us not to forget one more thing—love. "And regardless of what else you put on, wear *love*. It's your basic, all-purpose garment. Never be without it" (Colossians 3:14 MSG).

Wow! I'd better check *the* list, re-pack, and change my tune to: *"We're marching to Zion, Beautiful, beautiful Zion; we're marching upward to Zion, The beautiful city of God."* [1]

✓ REALITY CHECK

Do you worry more about what is on the outside than the inside? Let your light shine so that all will see who your Master Designer truly is. Then on the red carpet, when asked who your designer is, you can boldly proclaim, "Jesus!"

⌛ PRAYER PAUSE

Lord, there are days I am overly concerned about how I look and how people see me. There are days that I cut people off on the freeway and talk down to the store clerk. Oh Father, make me more like You and help me to put on Your love, mercy, kindness, humility, gentleness, and patience.

✱ FOOTNOTES

1. Written by Isaac Watts, 1707. Music by Robert Lowry. Public Domain.

THA-THUMP

Don't you just love the spring season? Crocuses and daffodils lead the floral seasonal parade followed closely by tulips and lilacs. They remind us that winter is gone and spring has *sprung*...or at least that's how it's supposed to happen. As I look at the calendar on the wall, it says April, but the weather around here is beating to the sound of a different drummer. April showers bring May flowers, right? Answer me this—how can the temperature be 82 degrees with a beautiful blue sky one day, and snowing the next? Very strange indeed. Today, the weatherman predicted snow on the valley floor. That's us! It's mid-April! Doesn't the weather understand that our snow tires have been stowed away until *next* winter?

Along with the removal of the winter tires comes the arrival of an unwelcome sight. Ruts! Potholes! Those nasty holes in the road that seem to pop up (or sink down) every spring. You can be driving down the road, sailing along on the smooth surface, and boom! Pothole! You usually feel the rut before you even see it. Or you see it way too late to avoid it. Thump, thump!

Isn't that like life? Potholes and ruts come at us constantly. Things are going great and boom! Out of nowhere—a pothole. Jesus told us that in this life we would hit many potholes. Well, sort of. He said, "In this world you will have trouble. But take heart! I have overcome the world" (John 16:33 NIV). *The Message* says, "In this godless world you will continue to experience difficulties." Boy howdy! Thanks for the warning!

I have to remember that when I go through the potholes of life that I'm not going through them alone. Jeremiah 30:11 assures us, "For I am with you and will save you, says the LORD."

Luke 3:5 says "Fill in the valleys, and level the mountains and hills! Straighten the curves, and smooth out the rough places!" Not only do the potholes and ruts need to be filled in and smoothed out, so do our lives. We know trials will come. Jesus flashed that warning light.

Isaiah also warned us about potholes and ruts. He said: "When you go through deep waters and great trouble, I will be with you. When you go through rivers of difficulty, you will not drown! When you walk through the fire of oppression, you will not be burned up; the flames will not consume you" (Isaiah 43:2). He didn't say *if*, he said *when*. Chances are every one of us will hit a pothole at some time in our life. Yet when we hit them, we need to continue *through* them—same as the difficulties we face daily.

I've been reminded recently, the hard way, of a lesson I should never forget. Armor up! I had gotten a bit lazy and forgot just how much I need to put on the armor of God each day—to ask for protection from evil and from potholes.

The armor is found in Ephesians 6:11–18. Paul tells us to: "Put on all of God's armor so that you will be able to stand firm against all strategies and tricks of the Devil. For we are not fighting against people made of flesh and blood, but against the evil rulers and authorities of the unseen world, against those mighty powers of darkness who rule this world, and against wicked spirits in the heavenly realms.

"Use every piece of God's armor to resist the enemy in the time of evil, so that after the battle you will still be standing firm. Stand your ground, putting on the sturdy belt of truth [to fight Satan's lies with God's truth] and the body armor of God's righteousness [to protect our heart]. For shoes, put on the peace that comes from the Good News, so that you will be fully prepared [get walking, spread God's Word]. In every battle you will need faith as your shield to stop the fiery arrows aimed at you by Satan [deflect those arrows, Wonder Woman]. Put on salvation as your helmet [protect that mind of yours from doubting God], and take the sword of the Spirit, which is the word of God [the only offensive weapon on the list and Satan cringes when the name of Jesus is spoken]. Pray at all times and on every occasion in the power of the Holy Spirit. Stay alert and be persistent in your prayers for all Christians everywhere."

Potholes come, potholes go (hopefully). We get in ruts, we get out (hopefully). Some are of our own making; some are not. Whatever...be on guard. Be prepared and armor up!

✓ **REALITY CHECK**

Seems like life is like a pothole, you never know when you are going to hit one! Life is going well and then, thump. Keep your eyes on the road, on Jesus. You might still hit a bump in the road, but you have Someone with you.

⌛ **PRAYER PAUSE**

Jesus, there are days when it seems everything I do lands me in a pothole. Help me to be aware of where they are as I maneuver through life. I pray those thumps in life will cause me to be alert and never take my eyes off You.

IT'S ABOUT ATTITUDE

What do a Steller's blue jay, a brown rabbit, a gray squirrel, and 50 women have in common? Not much you say? I would have thought that too, until I witnessed it firsthand.

I was speaking at a women's retreat in Zephyr Point, Nevada, at a beautiful Presbyterian Church retreat center 6,509 feet above sea level in the Sierra Nevada Mountains. The facility overlooks the second deepest lake in the United States at 1,645 feet—Lake Tahoe. The lake straddles the states of California and Nevada where the area is such a contrast between nature and man. Nature, with its beautiful lake and magnificent snowcapped mountains, complete with the sun casting a ray of light across the lake as it sets behind those mountains. You'll find endless hiking trails and downhill ski runs. Contradicting that picture and to the south of the retreat center, just around the bend, are the gambling casinos of Stateline, Nevada. Beauty and the beast I guess. Nature vs. nickels.

During the conference, we were singing one of the rich traditional hymns of the church. As a kid, I remember our chancel choir singing this song as they processed down the center aisle of the church in their red robes. Now you may prefer the newer contemporary praise songs, but when "Holy! Holy! Holy! Lord God Almighty" is being sung, look out! It's powerful. It was during this song that I saw something amazing. Just as we sang the line "All Thy works shall praise Thy name in earth and sky and sea"[1] a Steller's jay flew onto a nearby tree limb and appeared to be looking at us, perhaps wondering what was going on inside the conference center. Then, a rabbit cautiously hopped close to the window and peered in. All thy works...birds, rabbits, and humans, all wanting in on the praise of our God.

As if that wasn't a big enough glimpse of God, the cake was about to be iced when my eyes went to a squirrel just outside the window. I watched its journey across the lawn. Walk a few steps and stop; walk a few steps and stop. Over and over. And with each stopping, the little critter's paws came up to its face—almost like hands folded in prayer. Walk, stop, and pray. Walk, stop and pray.

God's message to me was to pray continually or as 1 Thessalonians 5:18 says, "Keep on praying." Walk a little, stop a little...and talk a lot—to God.

We are to "pray at all times and on every occasion in the power of the Holy Spirit" (Ephesians 6:18).

Paul is reminding us to keep a prayerful attitude—an attitude of gratitude, thankfulness, and a constant awareness of who God is and that He is always with us. Pray constantly, pray often, and keep your focus on God. Oh, and pray when you don't feel like it. Pray without ceasing.

So, the beauty of God's creation? It was...

"Indescribable! Uncontainable!
You placed the stars in the sky, And You know them by name;
You are amazing, God!
All-powerful! Untamable! Awestruck, we fall to our knees
As we humbly proclaim: You are amazing, God!"[2]

Oh, and just to remind me He was still in charge...an earthquake struck, waking me up at 4:00 a.m. Oh yeah...I hear You, God! Not only that, I feel Your presence!

For sure! Forever! Amen!

✓ REALITY CHECK

Do you have an attitude of gratitude and thankfulness? Pray! Focus on God. Give thanks.

⧗ PRAYER PAUSE

You created all things Father. Thank You for those "catch-a-glimpse" of You moments, through Your creation. Your Word says, "Let everything that has breath praise the Lord" (Psalm 150:6 NIV).

✽ FOOTNOTES

1. Reginald Heber 1826 Public Domain
2. Words and Music by Laura Story; Additional Lyrics by Jesse Reeves © 2004 worshiptogether.com Songs/six steps Music/Gleaning Publishing (all rights adm. EMI CMG Publishing)

CERTAINTIES

Benjamin Franklin once said, "In this world nothing can be said to be certain, except death and taxes." I beg to differ.

As I write, my son Matt is in South America. His two-month adventure is taking him to four countries, meeting with pastors and church leaders, discussing the growth of Christianity on that continent.

His car has been parked at my mom's since he's been gone. My husband decided it should be driven to keep the battery charged and asked, "Do *you* have some time to take it for a spin?" It was then I knew there were other certainties in life besides death and taxes.

First certainty: I would be able to find at least one empty Starbucks cup in his car. And the second certainty: The gas gauge would be on "E." Some things never change!

Needless to say that in order to charge the battery, I had to charge my card—my gas card. I put $15 worth of gas in the car which equaled just a little over three gallons. I remember the days when $3 could buy 15 gallons of gas! Out of spite, I just might drive the car while he's gone, leaving the tank in the condition I found it—dry!

Life provides changes and uncertainties all the time: Smooth skin to wrinkles, firm underarms to the flying flesh, hair on your head to hair, well, not on your head. Are you there yet?

What was touted as a wonderful discovery more than 50 years ago, is now old hat. Watching *Bonanza* in "living color" at my grandparents' house was a big deal when I was a kid. We even liked it when the peacock, the symbol for "in living color," opened its plume. Now color is not just color, it's HD and who knows what else. A black-and-white TV is a thing of the past. Computers, tablets, and cell phone are up-dated yearly. How do we keep up?

I have found there is only one certainty in life, one constant, one thing we can count on to never change and that is Jesus Christ. He-brews 13:8 says, "Jesus Christ is the same yesterday, today, and forever."

The author of Hebrews said Jesus never changes. So why do people try to re-create Him? We are the ones who need to be new creations (2 Corinthians 5:17), not Jesus.

God's Word never changes either. Oh, we try to change it. We've translated and paraphrased the Bible into so many versions that it's los-ing the original meaning of the text. We've watered scripture down to how we want it to read—what we want it to say. God's plan of salvation is still the same today, as it was yesterday, as it will be tomorrow...ac-knowledge, confess repent, accept. "For if you confess with your mouth that Jesus is Lord and believe in your heart that God raised him from the dead, you will be saved" (Romans 10:9). There is still only one way to heaven, even though some people want to believe many roads lead there. Where does scripture say that? John 14:6 clearly says, "I am the way, the truth, and the life. No one can come to the Father *except through* me." Sorry, I guess I'm pretty black and white here—no variations on a theme.

How many certainties are in your life? One egg in the fridge when the recipe calls for three? No sugar when you need one-half cup? Out of milk when you want cereal? The stoplights are all red when you're running late? Doesn't it just figure? But that's life, and life changes. The only thing in life that changes is life itself. That, you can depend on.

It's true that life will always bring death and taxes. That may indeed be certain. But the only thing that is worth depending on—that never changes, is always certain and constant—is Jesus. Count on it.

✓ REALITY CHECK

God's Word never changes, yet the world keeps trying to reinvent it and water it down. Stand firm on the Word of God, not the way of the world.

⧗ PRAYER PAUSE

Father God, Your Word says, "God's solid foundation stands firm" (2 Timothy 2:19 NIV). When faced with temptation from the world, help me to stand firm on the Word, even in the face of ridicule or persecution.

16

WAR PAINT

I recently returned from Orlando, Florida, the "other" home of Mickey Mouse. I was there attending the International Christian Retail Show to promote my second book. It was a fast-paced, fun-filled week of TV and radio interviews, signing books, and having tea with Mickey and Carol. Carol McCallum went with me as my business manager, publicist, encourager, keeper, and best friend...and we had a blast! (What happens in Orlando stays in Orlando!)

My interview with *The Good Life Orlando* TV program started with a bang. First up...makeup! That's right. Step right up, sit right down. Gina, the makeup artist, performed her magic on my face, covering up the shiny spots, which prepared me to sit under the hot lights of the TV set.

What a thrill for me! I sat down and looked into a mirror surrounded by those little round light bulbs, like you see in movie star's dressing rooms. I felt like Maria from the Broadway play, *West Side Story* when she sang, "I feel pretty, oh so pretty" and "See the pretty girl in that mirror there? Who can that attractive girl be?" [1]

I've never had my makeup *done*. I'm pretty basic in most things I do, and the less time it takes to complete the beauty make-over, the better.

Growing up, I didn't do many girlie things. I'd rather be playing baseball with the boys or climbing trees than playing dolls with the girls or learning to sew.

Paint my fingernails? No way! I had no use for that. And my hair? Keep it short and pixie style. No time to style it, just blow it dry and call it good. Oh how things change.

As I write, my hair is styled, or at least I called it styled, with blonde highlights (thank you Carol) and my fingernails *and* toenails are painted. My morning lipstick had worn off after two cups of coffee, so I've applied more. If my friends could see me now.

While all of this is fun, new and exciting, God's Word tells us that true beauty begins on the inside.

"What matters is not your outer appearance—the styling of your hair, the jewelry you wear, the cut of your clothes—but your inner disposition. Cultivate inner beauty, the gentle, gracious kind that God delights in" (1 Peter 3:3-4 MSG).

Sometimes it seems we just put on a face found in a jar and call it good. It's not the changed hairdo, the painted nails, or the painted face that makes an impression on God—or anyone else for that matter. It's Christ living within you...beauty on the inside. And that beauty should radiate with the love of Jesus Christ.

While the makeup camouflaged my face from the glare of the lights, there is no amount of makeup than can cover an empty or hurting heart. I know. You can't fake it with God.

It's your heart that God looks at. It's where the true beauty of a person lies. Yet sometimes we can't get past the outer wrapping to see the real beauty of a person. People look at us differently when we are overweight. I know. They look at us differently when we get older. I know that too, I'm afraid. We pick beauty over the beast because it looks better from our worldly eyes, only to realize God is right: Outward beauty is only skin deep. And outward beauty doesn't last.

"A voice said, 'Shout!'

"I asked, 'What should I shout?'

"'Shout that people are like the grass that dies away. Their beauty fades as quickly as the beauty of flowers in a field. The grass withers, and the flowers fade beneath the breath of the LORD. And so it is with people. The grass withers, and the flowers fade, but the word of our God stands forever'" (Isaiah 40:6–8).

As the saying goes, don't judge a book by its cover—and don't judge a person by their cover.

REALITY CHECK

God looks at what's on the inside of a person, at their heart. Do you?

⧗ PRAYER PAUSE

Lord, help me to see people with Your eyes, with Your heart. Proverbs 31:30 reminds us that "Charm is deceptive, and beauty does not last." Help me to take time to see the beauty on the inside of people and to not be quick to judge or dismiss a person by how they look on the outside.

✳ FOOTNOTES

1. Music by Leonard Bernstein, lyrics by Stephen Sondheim. © 1956, 1957 Amberson Holdings LLC and Stephen Sondheim. Copyright renewed. Leonard Bernstein Music Publishing Company LLC, Publisher

STRAIGHT AHEAD!

We bikers have an unspoken tradition when meeting each other on the road. It doesn't matter if the machine is a big Harley hog, or a little piglet zoom-zoom scooter. We always give that special sign of recognition—a wave. Not a big hand wave, just a subtle, hand to the side, slight movement, almost like a nod. Yes we are a special breed.

I love speeding down the road on my scooter. Well, speeding for me is 35 mph (40 if I push it). That's as fast as my scooter will go. The manufacturer pre-set the limit.

Riding a scooter is obviously more dangerous than driving a car. You don't have the protection a car provides, but then, you don't have as much fun either! There's just something about bugs in your teeth that I cannot begin to describe. (You are welcome!)

One lesson riding a scooter has taught me: Pay attention and keep my eyes on the road. Any long glances to the side of the road and the scooter might just follow the glance. Not good when a car is coming from the opposite direction! Also, use the side mirrors. Turning my head around to check out what's behind me won't turn me into a pillar of salt, but it could send me flying into the ditch—or worse. When I take my eyes off the road, danger lurks. You never know when a car will swerve in your direction, or a dog, cat or even a humanoid will run out into your path. Then there is the bug that will go splat on your face. There's no room for daydreaming; you must focus and concentrate.

Peter tells us about the dangers of not keeping our eyes on the road. In 1 Peter 5:8–9 we hear, "Be careful! Watch out for attacks from the Devil, your great enemy. He prowls around like a roaring lion, looking for some victim to devour. Take a firm stand against him, and be strong in your faith."

He says: Keep Your Eyes on the Road.

Before I hit the road on my scooter, I do what I can to protect myself. I put on a jacket, sunglasses, helmet and gloves. And I expect the unexpected. The scooter will perform without any of the gear I wear, but I won't hit the streets without it. I know I need to armor up—to protect myself.

God's Word says the same thing—that we need to protect ourselves or armor up! "Use every piece of God's armor to resist the enemy in the time of evil, so that after the battle you will still be standing firm. Stand your ground, putting on the sturdy belt of truth and the body armor of God's righteousness" (Ephesians 6:13–14).

Just like I put on my safety equipment to ride my scooter, every day we need to put on our own safety equipment. Those items, found in Ephesians 6, are: the belt of truth, the body armor of righteousness, shoes to spread the Good News, shield of faith, helmet of salvation, and the sword, which is the Word of God.

We can't resist the enemy without God's help, without weapons, without protection. And pray in the power that He has given us!

As I said, my scooter has its limits, set by the manufacturer. No matter how badly I want my scooter to keep up with the big *hogs*, it can't. I have limits set for me too, just like my scooter does. Oh I hear "the world is limitless," but I usually end up in the ditch—black and blue, if I listen to the call of the world.

I can't push my scooter past its limits and God's Word says we will never be pushed past our limits. God, as our manufacturer, has set those limits. "He'll never let you be pushed past your limit; he'll always be there to help you come through it" (1 Corinthians 10:13 MSG).

So to avoid the ditches of life, follow the speed limit set by God, and armor up with your protective gear, issued by your *manufacturer*—the belt, the body armor, the shoes, the helmet. And carry your sword. Equipment guaranteed by God. Don't leave home without Him.

✓ REALITY CHECK

Do you push the limits? Be careful!

⧖ PRAYER PAUSE

Father God, help me to remember to run the race You set for me, at the pace You set. And keep my eyes focused on the road You are clearing for me.

FOLLOW THE LEADER

I've never been much of a dancer. It's a timing thing. Clapping my hands in rhythm is a challenge, let alone keeping my body moving to the beat of the music. Musically, my mind and body do not want to work together and I'm afraid "feeling" the music doesn't exist for me.

So when my son Matt and his buddy Brad were goofing off in the back of the church sanctuary one day, dancing *together* as Hector (the foreign exchange student who was living with Brad and his family) played the piano, why in the world would I cut in? I ask you, why in the world would I cut in? It was like a scene out of the musical "The King and I" where Anna was trying to teach the King of Siam how to dance. She was singing, "Shall we dance?" and between the lyrics of the song, he was saying, "One, two, three, and? One, two three, and?" The king was following her lead, until he got it! And then around the room they danced, up and over the furniture, around and around. And..."again!" he says.

Matt took my right hand in his left and put his other hand on my waist—and tried to take the lead. He wanted to do a box step and I didn't want to box, I wanted to waltz. He tried to control me, and the stubborn mule that I am (now really ready to *box*), balked. Finally exasperated, he said, "Mom, let me lead!"

How many times have I heard my Jesus say that to me? "Barb, let Me lead!" Yet I proceed full speed ahead without Him.

As I read scripture, I've yet to find where Jesus said He would follow me. "*He leads* me beside quiet waters" (Psalm 23:2 NIV). "Show me the path where I should walk, O LORD; point out the right road for *me to follow*" (Psalm 25:4).

John clearly tells us who should be doing the leading and who should be doing the following in chapter 10, verses 3–4 of his gospel. We read that the Shepherd leads and we follow. And adds, "*if* we know His voice!" "The gatekeeper opens the gate for him, and the sheep hear his voice and come to him. He calls his own sleep by name and leads them out. After he has gathered his own flock, he walks ahead of them, and they follow him because they recognize his voice."

I remember back in the 60s, Little Peggy March sang a song about following a boy, with the lyrics, "I will follow him, follow him wherever he may go."[1] Thirty years later, the movie *Sister Act* re-introduced that song to the world. Difference being, the "I will follow Him" was talking about God.

He wants us to put our hand in His and allow Him to put His arms around our waist, allowing Him to lead the dance…yet we balk because we can't hear the music. We can't hear Him. We only hear the sound of our own voice.

God needs people who will take the lead here on earth to do His work. And He needs those who will follow the leaders He has chosen. But even leading requires following—following Jesus.

Dancing might require a partner who hears the beat with which to lead, but we always need to follow the lead of the One who has been there, done that, and has great rhythm.

✓ REALITY CHECK

Which music do you listen to? The subtle sound of your own voice, the loud sound of the world, or the truth in the Word of God?

⧗ PRAYER PAUSE

"Teach me your way, O Lord, and I will walk in your truth; give me an undivided heart, that I may fear your name" (Psalm 86:11 NIV).

⧉ FOR THE RECORD

Membership in my club is still open...G.A.G (Getting Ahead of God)

✱ FOOTNOTES

1. English lyrics by Norman Gimbel. Jacques Plante original song in French.

DOMINO EFFECT

Today has been rush, rush, rush. And because of it, it seems that every one of my actions has caused a reaction. Reach for a paper, a stack nearby falls. Pick them up; hit my head on the desk. Make a pot of coffee, and forget to put the pot under the dripping water. Clean up the water, and soak my shirt. Empty the coffee grounds and drop them on the floor. Sweep up the grounds and knock over the garbage. Pick up the garbage and my back catches. As the old saying goes, "The hurrier I go, the behinder I get." Why does this happen to me when I don't have time for delays?

I skip lunch and stay late—hurry, hurry, hurry. Gotta get things done. After work, I drove into Vancouver to pick up supplies for the women's conference. First stop, Costco. Picked up what was on my list. Second stop, Walmart, to check out the flowers. Third stop was Winco, another grocery store, to purchase things not found at the other stores. I had crossed off everything on my list except one item—orange juice. As I headed to the orange juice cooler, the loudspeaker announced, "Please evacuate the store due to a fire." What? I need orange juice! I thought I could sneak past the store employee who was ushering people out. No such luck. Seems the fire was right across from—of all places—the orange juice. So I headed to the front of the store and was told to leave my cart and exit the building. What? I can't at least pay for what I have? The answer was no! I had just spent over an hour in the store and was leaving empty-handed.

The fire trucks were just pulling up, so I knew this was going to be a longer wait than I wanted to stick around for. So I got in my car and headed to the Winco on the other side of town, driving through Mc-Donald's on the way. Remember, I'd skipped lunch, so I was starving! I ate my food so fast I felt sick! And of course, spilled half of it in my lap.

I felt like Alexander, the character in the Judith Viorst book who had a "terrible, horrible, no good, very bad day," [1] and thought he'd move to Australia. I was ready to pack!

My journey through the new Winco was of course, without my shopping list. It was in the cart I had abandoned at the other store. So I was shopping by memory (not a good thing to do). As I was fuming my way around the store, I was hit full in the face by you know who—God.

From Him I heard, "This is the day that the LORD has made. We *will* rejoice and be glad in it" (Psalm 118:24). The absolute last thing I wanted to do was rejoice or be glad—about anything! It was then that He opened the eyes of my heart. Here I was in a grocery store, with shelves loaded down with food. The store was warm, had lights, refrigeration, and...a bathroom. I had money to pay for what was in my cart, gas in my car (oh yeh, I had a car!), a healthy body to walk around the store, eyes to see, ears to hear, and, though it might be debatable, a sound mind.

I had a whole lot to be thankful for. James 1:2 tells us, "Whenever trouble comes your way, let it be an opportunity for joy." When-ever, not *if*-ever. (Argh! I knew I should have used my *"black* hi-lighter" on that verse.)

I was worried about details again. My anxiousness was self-inflict-ed. Everything would come together, I knew that. Yet I fretted...and then I fumed. Philippians 4:6–7 reminds us, "Do not be anxious about anything, but in *everything*, by prayer and petition, with thanksgiving, present your requests to God. And the peace of God, which transcends all understanding, will guard your hearts and your minds in Christ Jesus" (NIV).

I didn't have the peace because I was anxious and I had not prayed once that day. Not once! It was past time, to stop, drop, and pray.

Jesus tells us in John 16:33, "In this world you will have trouble. But take heart! I have overcome the world!" (NIV). He said we would have struggles and trials, but we don't go through them alone. He is there with us all the way.

Thank You, Jesus, for the reminder. I have so much to be thankful for. One of these days, I just might get it!

Oh...and Alexander? At the end of the book, his mother reminded him that even people in Australia have bad days.

✓ REALITY CHECK

Are you anxious today? Feeling burdened and overwhelmed? Have you chatted with God about it? Go to Him now.

⧖ PRAYER PAUSE

Jesus, forgive me for not sharing my burdens with You, for taking on too much and working myself into an anxious state. Replace my anxious and troubled heart and mind with Your perfect peace.

✱ FOOTNOTES

1. © 1972 Judith Viorst

PECKING AWAY

How much wood can a woodpecker peck, if a woodpecker could peck wood? Okay, so that's not how the saying goes, but that is my immediate question! Maybe I should ask, "How long can a woodpecker peck until the woodpecker's pecking drives me crazy?" I have an answer to that question—not long!

I truly believe that all creatures need to do what they need to do in order to survive. I just don't like it when their need interferes with *my* need and *my* need is for peace and quiet! I've banged on the window to get it to stop. I've gone outside in the pouring-down rain and yelled at the bird. He flies away, and as soon as I turn around, he's back at it! Peck, peck, peck. Why doesn't he get it? He is in my space!

The fact is, I've still got a pretty good throwing arm and the thought of throwing a rock at the annoying bird has entered my mind. However, missing it also entered my mind and I'm not quite sure how I would explain to the Schurmans how I broke the upper window of their house at Hood Canal. "Well, you see, this bird was annoying me..."

The bird is not interested in the bark from trees surrounding this house, because that wouldn't bug me. He is interested in the wood siding *on* the house. Bug me? Funny thing...that is what the bird wants—bugs.

It's looking for food (and a mate!). It is simply trying to survive.

There is another rat-tat-tat this week that I've been hearing. It breaks the silence, and is only *heard* in the silence. It's the voice of God. God's Word tells us that Jesus stands at the door and knocks. Revelation 3:20 reminds us that He is asking us to open the door to our heart and let Him come in. But we get so distracted by the things of the world, by the noises, that we can't hear His knock. And the door to our heart stays shut, locked.

For years, I thought that verse was talking to those who didn't believe in Jesus, and perhaps on one level, it is. However that verse is dead smack in the middle of the letter written to the church of Laodicea, a church that had been happy with the way things were. No changes, good or bad. No moving ahead, no moving backwards. Stagnant. Jesus was giving them a wake-up call, and He's giving us one too. We can't be happy doing things the way we've always done them. With each generation that comes behind us, their way of doing things the way we've always done them is going to be different than ours. Whose way is better? Whose standard do we follow? I can answer that one too. God's way, God's standard!

On the chance of sounding narrow-minded, God's way is the only way. Jesus said, "I am the way and the truth and the life. No one comes to the Father except through me" (John 14:6 NIV). The way to God is through Jesus. It's not through the decorations, the color of the paint, the pictures on the wall, the bells ringing at noon, candles, the music, or the sermon. They may all point you to Jesus, but they are not *the* way.

Maybe you have lost your way? Maybe you've taken a wrong turn or a detour. Maybe you've hit a bump in the road or maybe you can't decide which direction God is calling you to go. Maybe you need to do like I'm doing right now...take time away from the noise. Maybe you will hear an annoying woodpecker or maybe you will hear the gentle voice of Jesus that comes in a whisper.

God spoke to Elijah in 1 Kings 19. There was a windstorm, but the LORD was not in the windstorm. There was an earthquake, but He wasn't there either. Then came fire and again God was not in it. Finally, a gentle whisper. God's voice was heard in the silence. (My paraphrase.)

I had to step away from the world, from the noises, to hear God. Maybe He came in the woodpecker, or the geese flying overhead, or the rain beating against the house. They all certainly got my attention. And then, the electricity went out—no lights, no TV, no internet, and no hot tea. It was me and God, alone at last. When I wouldn't turn off the distractions of the world, He did it for me. It was God and me... One on one.

Open God's Word. Quietly read it. And listen for His voice in the silence. You will be amazed at just how *loud* it really is.

✓ REALITY CHECK

If the world is rat-a-tat-tatting in your space, turn it off and tune into God. You will hear His still, small voice in the quietness, not the chaos.

⧗ PRAYER PAUSE

Speak to me, Jesus. Your servant is listening.

WALKING THE TALK

The TV news stations are calling it "The Arctic Blast." Reporters are telling us this is the worst snowstorm since 1968, and one news anchor said, "You old-timers will remember that." Ouch! I'm afraid that means me!

I stuck a ruler into the snow on my deck, and the measurement reached the 10-inch mark. A snowdrift at the side of my house is almost as high as the fence. A tree branch in my front yard is covered with so much snow that it has drooped to the ground, brushing the deep snow. I've been holed up in the house all day. I couldn't get out if I wanted to...the snow in my driveway is higher than the underside of my car. (Wondering if my scooter would make it?) Are we having fun yet?

On Saturday, my son Matt, who was living in Portland, ventured north (in the snow) from Portland to Woodland for a birthday party. Unbeknownst to me, I called his cell phone about the time he was talking to a State Patrol trooper, about three miles south of here. Seems Matt had stopped to help a woman whose car was stuck in the snow...and lo and behold, Matt also became stuck. My first response was "What in the world are you doing out on a day like today?" Second response was, "What were you thinking about by pulling to the side of the freeway?"

Answer to question one: He wanted to celebrate with his friends.

Answer to number two: He simply wanted to help someone in trouble. It was the answer to number two that I had a hard time arguing with.

In Luke 10:25–27, a religious leader asked Jesus a question: "What must I do to receive eternal life?" To answer that question, Jesus asked him what the law said, and the man responded: "'You must love the Lord your God with all your heart, all your soul, all your strength, and all your mind.' And, 'Love your neighbor as yourself.'"

Jesus follows that statement with a story about a Jewish man on a trip. Instead of being sidetracked by snow, he met up with bandits who took his clothes and his money and beat him up. They left him alongside the road.

What happened next amazes me. No one stopped to help him! A priest saw him and crossed to the other side of the road. A temple assistant stopped, looked at him, and walked on. They saw him, and did nothing! Finally a Samaritan came by. Jews and Samaritans hated each other. Yet it was the Samaritan who stopped...and helped the man. The religious leaders didn't help. *The religious leaders didn't help!*

Each one had their own agenda. Places to go, people to meet, things to do. They didn't have time for a stranger, let alone a stranger they hated. Matt had a destination in mind, traveling through the snow, but he made time for a stranger, and it cost him. The woman he had pulled off to help had been waiting for more than two hours for help. Everyone passed her by. Thanks to her cell phone, help was on the way...when they could get there. While Matt couldn't get her out of the snow, and became stuck himself, he did provide something. He provided care, concern, and love. The love of Jesus...the Golden Rule, "Do for others what you would like them to do for you" (Matthew 7:12).

I'd like to think I would have taken the time to stop, to get out of my car, get wet, get cold, and get stuck in the snow to help a stranger. But I bet I wouldn't do it. I'd leave that for someone else, for someone else, for someone else.

The question is: Who is my neighbor? And the answer is: Anyone who needs your help, no matter what the color of their skin or the country of their birth. No matter if they are old or young, rich or poor. The kind of love Jesus talked about transcends all of this. The kind of love Jesus talked about is love in action. Do you have that kind of love? I wish I did.

We can say we love someone, but when push comes to shove, do we? Do we just talk it and not walk it. The religious expert said we were to "love our neighbor as yourself"...and then didn't walk it.

Matt talked it, stopped, and walked it. Way to go, Matt. I've a lot to learn from you.

The TV news today was full of Good Samaritan stories...and using that exact title. People are bringing food to travelers stranded at the airport; blankets to the cold and weary people at the train and bus stations. Sometimes it seems that in the worst of times, it brings out the best in people—sometimes.

"Do to others what you would have them to do to you" (Matthew 7:12 NIV). Words to live by; words to put into action.

✓ REALITY CHECK

Do your beliefs match your actions? If you're going to talk it, you have to walk it.

⌛ PRAYER PAUSE

Lord, I pray that I don't copy the actions of those religious leaders who were so busy being religious that they failed to do the work of God. Help me to remember that my actions speak louder than words and that what I do is based on Whose I am.

HOPE

It finally happened. I knew the day would come; I just didn't think it would be *this* soon. The day has arrived when I am older than the President of the United States.

When did I grow so old?

The buzz phrases I've heard throughout the winning campaign have been "Change is coming" and "Yes, we can."

People are talking about how they have a new sense of hope. Young people voted like never before. They became involved in the grassroots campaign, knocking on doors, attending rallies, and having conversations over coffee and beer about politics.

Change...hope...yes, we can.

While I truly believe things are going to change, some for the good—some for the not-so-good—I have to remember that a new president, no matter how excited we get about the ideas and goals put forth, is not the true agent for change or for hope.

I thought about hope, and how people have placed their hope in this mortal man. Must be a heavy burden for someone to carry.

Do yourself a favor. Please don't place all your hope and dreams in a mere man. For a man will disappoint you at some point. We have to stop and remember that our only hope for this world is not a man but *the* man—God in the flesh—Jesus Christ. He is the *only* hope for this sin-filled world. The burden is on His shoulders. Jesus came not as the great white hope, or the great black hope. He is the *only* hope for the world.

During the 2008 presidential election, people were divided on the candidates: Democrats vs. Republicans; liberals vs. conservatives. And yet in the end, we knew that only one person would be left standing after the vote was tallied. And it might not be the candidate we backed.

But wasn't that true in Jesus' time? We had the Pharisees on one side, following God to the letter of the law. Then we had those on the other side, following Jesus, God in human form, and the spirit of the law—the fulfillment of the law.

And I wondered. What kind of world would this be if all who got involved in politics, working as agents of change, would get as involved and that excited about promoting Jesus?

How would it be if they continuously spoke His name? If they attended rallies, invited people to church, and spouted His platform every chance they got? What if they were so convincing that they got the unbelievers to vote for Jesus? To jump on board and to accept Jesus as Lord and Savior?

Scripture is filled with the answer to our hope:

"And so, Lord, where do I put my hope? My only hope is in you" (Psalm 39:7).
"O Lord, you alone are my hope" (Psalm 71:5).
"My only hope is in him" (Isaiah 8:17).
"Blessed are those who trust in the Lord and have made the Lord their hope and confidence" (Jeremiah 17:7).

"And if you are asked about your Christian hope, always be ready to explain it" (1 Peter 3:15).

It appears to me that it's easier to share why we have hope in one candidate over another than it is to share where our true hope comes from. We know inside and out where our candidate stands on the issues. Do we know what God's Word says about the issues? Do we know His platform? Why can we put a political bumper sticker on the back of our car but not a fish proclaiming we are Christians?

What would happen if we placed our hope and our trust in one man—in Christ alone? I'll tell you—the world would change.

"In Christ alone my hope is found, He is my light, my strength, my song. This Cornerstone, This solid ground, Firm through the fiercest drought and storm." [1]

✓ REALITY CHECK

"He has given us his very great and precious promises" (2 Peter 1:4 NIV). Where does your hope lie? Stand firm on the promises of God.

⧗ PRAYER PAUSE

"My hope is built on nothing less, than Jesus' blood and righteousness." [2]

▭ FOR THE RECORD

On November 4, 2008, Barack Obama was elected as the 44th President of the United States. He was 47 years old at the time of the election.

✱ FOOTNOTES

1. Words and Music by Stuart Townsend and Keith Getty © 2002 Thank you Music
2. Words by Edward Mote. Public Domain

DIG IN

When I looked out the window this morning, the water was calm. This is the first day it's been smooth sailing since I've been at Hood Canal. The water was not angry, but at peace. Last night, the waves were pounding against the rocks; one wave after another came crashing to the shore—up and over the concrete seawall.

Hours later, as I write, the storm is raging outside and I could care less. I find it invigorating! But then, I'm sitting in a warm and cozy house, sipping hot tea. The biggest decision I have to make today is whether or not I get dressed (not!).

A madrone tree growing just outside my window has caught my eye. I give it the once over, twice over, and then become fascinated with the little tree. Its roots are firmly planted on the side of the steep cliff with its branches hanging out over the rocky beach below. The tree is being battered by the wind and rain, and yet it stands firm. Tall fir trees on each side of the madrone sway in the wind, some losing their branches. But the madrone endures the strong winds.

Madrone trees always catch my attention. There is something so *familiar* about them.

These trees are native to the Pacific Northwest, especially along the coastline. There are no blossoms on the tree right now—it's out of season. What I love about this tree, with its fighting spirit, is what lies under its rough, paper-thin bark. I know from past adventures, that the bark is rough to the touch, yet easily peels away in strips (kind of like the skin from a sunburn!). Beneath that rough exterior layer you will discover very smooth bark—I'm talking baby-bottom smooth. I love to run my hand down the protected wood. It is the exact opposite of the outer layer...rough vs. smooth. You'd never know the smooth interior was there by its rough protective exterior. To get to the smooth interior, you have to peel back the outer bark.

What I love most about those familiar trees is the reflection I see in them. I see me. I am so like that tree. The madrone serves as a reminder to me...what to be and what not to be. I still wear a lot of my protective exterior. I still have walls up, to protect myself from the zingers that come at me. Some zingers manage to get through...and it hurts...and I retreat. Yet through the storms of life, I am so thankful that my roots are firmly planted in who I am, and Who I believe in. You'd be hard-pressed to uproot me (many have tried and failed!). While my feet are firmly planted in my Jesus, I also have this need to branch out...to test the water, or to grow toward it.

I did some *digging* into the madrone tree and have a whole new appreciation for them. They don't like having their roots disturbed. Do any of us? They also tend to have irregular growth forms. If you add irreverent to that, I'm totally pegged. They also become stunted and gnarled by the wind...but...if they aren't *stressed*, they thrive! (A tree gets stressed?)

But what about those roots? The wind has been whipping all week. The lights have flickered and gone out. (Cell phones, though there is no cell signal, make a great flashlight!) Through the storm, the madrone stands firm. And so will we if we have our roots firmly planted. And our roots need to be firmly planted in God's Word, so we can withstand the raging storms in our lives.

Colossians 2:6–7 says, "And now, just as you accepted Christ Jesus as your Lord, you must continue to live in obedience to him. Let your *roots grow down into him* and draw up nourishment from him, so you will grow in faith, strong and vigorous in the truth you were taught. Let your lives overflow with thanksgiving for all he has done."

The madrone tree has put down roots deep into the soil to withstand the storms. And we need to do the same thing: Put down roots into God's marvelous soil—His Word.

And once you've gotten your roots planted—beware. People, circumstances, or simply life will try to knock your feet, or your roots, out from under you.

"Don't let anyone lead you astray with empty philosophy and high-sounding nonsense that come from human thinking and from the evil powers of this world, and not from Christ" (Colossians 2:8).

Christ is our strength, our nourishment, our strong tower, our help in time of need. Dig in; grow down, so you can grow up.

And finally, we need to armor up and stand firm. "Use every piece of God's armor to resist the enemy in the time of evil, so that after the battle you will still be standing firm" (Ephesians 6:13).

We have two paths to follow. It's either the way of the Word, or the way of the world.

Which path will you take? Which has your attention, your devotion, your heart?

We are in a battle, whether we want to acknowledge it or not. Dig in. Hold on. Stand firm!

✓ REALITY CHECK

Are your roots firmly planted in God's Word so you can withstand what the world throws at you? Dig in!

⧗ PRAYER PAUSE

Father God, help me to hunker down when the storms of life blow my way. May my roots go down deep into Your marvelous soil so I will remain strong and firmly attached to You.

WHAT A TRIP

I have a *pet* peeve. Okay, so I have more than one. But number one on my list *right now*, is the click-click-click of our dog's nails on the wood floor. Drives me crazy!

I bought Snickers, our dog of 18 years, doggie paw slippers after we replaced our family room carpet with wood flooring. Now I have to put up with the annoying sound of him dragging his feet across the room with a plop-plop-plop. However, muted plop-plop-plop is much easier on my nerves than the sharp click-click-click.

Snickers hates these slippers. His hearing is long gone, but he can still run, and when I come after him with slippers in hand, he takes off for the door, sliding as he runs. I have learned to hide the slippers behind my back.

When I catch him, I lay him down and Velcro the leather muffs on his paws while I'm screaming, "You are driving me crazy!" (He can't hear, remember?)

Recently, I was down on my knees and had three out of four of the slippers on him when the phone rang. My husband and I were just preparing to sit down to dinner. (Isn't that when the phone usually rings?) At times like these, I tend to let the answering machine pick up the calls, or just check the caller ID. (Now you know!)

I remember standing up to go check the phone. The next thing I re-member was flat on my back on the floor whispering, "Don't touch me!"

It seems that when I stood to go check the phone, the nails on Snickers' remaining un-slippered paw got tangled up with my shoe-laces—you know, those extra-long shoelaces you have to double knot to keep from dragging on the floor? (Why *do* they make laces so long?) I was attached to the dog—he didn't like it, I didn't like it. Only I was the one who fell down and went boom! (Did you feel the earthquake?)

I was afraid to move, for fear some part of me wouldn't. My hus-band managed to untangle the dog's nails from my safety-hazard laces. He offered to help me up, but I just wanted to lie there on the hard floor, looking up at the ceiling.

Lesson? You fall down; you get back up. You might not trip on your own shoelaces. You might have suffered some other kind of setback in your life—family or finances, death or divorce. No matter what has tripped you up...get up! Reach out your hand and grab onto the hand of Jesus. "I waited patiently for the LORD to help me, and he turned to me and heard my cry. He lifted me out of the pit of despair, out of the mud and mire. He set my feet on solid ground and steadied me as I walked along" (Psalm 40:1–2).

Maybe something in your past is keeping you pinned to the mat. You are not down for the count. Let go of that "something" and latch on to Jesus. Psalm 37:24 says, "If he stumbles, he's not down for long; God has a grip on his hand" (MSG). Don't live in the past, live in the presence of Jesus. Remember this: Jesus is not the accuser. He is the forgiver.

I stumbled over my own shoelaces and fell over backwards...only to find myself looking up. And isn't that the way it should be? Some-times God allows us to fall or fail, so we *will* look up. Psalm 121:1–3 encourages us to look to God. "I look up to the mountains—does my help come from there? My help comes from the LORD, who made the heavens and the earth! He will not let you stumble and fall; the one who watches over you will not sleep.

"The LORD keeps you from all evil and preserves your life. The Lord keeps watch over you as you come and go, both now and forever" (Psalm 121:7–8). He's got you covered!

God is watching you, and not from a distance. Are your eyes focused on Him?

✓ REALITY CHECK

Falling doesn't mean failing. When you fall, look up and reach up. His hand is reaching out to you. Grab it!

⧗ PRAYER PAUSE

Father, why do I let minor irritations become major problems? Jesus, help me to focus on You—before I fall. Remind me that You are always there, waiting and watching. You never lose sight of me (or my shoelaces).

⬚ FOR THE RECORD

Snickers passed away shortly after this story was penned. He had a long life and was well loved.

ARE YOU READY?

The scene is predictable. We are getting ready to go somewhere and my husband asks, "What are you going to wear?"

"Not sure," I say. (I never know until the last minute.) Then he asks what *he* should wear, and I say, "Whatever you want." (I figure he's a big boy, he can pick out his own clothes.)

After hearing closet doors slam and the loud expulsion of human air, he comes out of the bedroom wearing a combination of clothes that leads me to believe he got dressed in the dark. "Is *that* what you're going to wear," I ask? In other words, "You aren't going to wear *that*, are you?" A *discussion* usually occurs and I end up saying, "Whatever."

Then I ask, "Are you ready to go?" The answer comes back from a voice sitting on the couch, working a crossword puzzle, "Whenever you are."

I don't know which is worse: getting ready, getting there, or being there!

The words "are you ready?" keep ringing in my ears. Barbara Mason asked that question in a song years ago. And the answer echoed back, "Yes, I'm ready."

But ready for what?

God's Word tells us to be ready—to be prepared. Matthew 24:42 says, "So be prepared, because you don't know what day your Lord is coming."

The headlines in the newspaper these days seem to speak of gloom and doom. Wars raging, nuclear testing, and piracy on the high seas. But this is nothing new. "And wars will break out near and far, but don't panic. Yes, these things must come, but the end won't follow immediately. The nations and kingdoms will proclaim war against each other, and there will be famines and earthquakes in many parts of the world" (Matthew 24:6–7).

Television cameras bring the disasters into our living room as they happen—in living color, high definition and surround sound—replaying the same scenes over and over again. It's almost as if we are there! We think the end must be near. Yet read the Old Testament. This is nothing new. There have always been wars and rumors of wars.

Larry Norman wrote a song about being ready. It says, "Life was filled with guns and war and everyone got trampled on the floor. I wish we'd all been ready." [1]

The question again is: "Are you ready?" I'm not asking if you're ready for tomorrow I'm asking, "Are you ready for eternity?"

Jesus tells us in Matthew 24:36, "No one knows the day or the hour when these things will happen, not even the angels in heaven or the Son himself. Only the Father knows."

Are you ready? Are you prepared? Preparation for anything is important. Even the Scout motto includes: "Be prepared."

We all want to look nice when attending an event. Going to a function at the Hilton ballroom probably calls for more than jeans, a T-shirt, and flip-flops. (Now you know my clothing style.)

Yet Jesus reminds us, "And why worry about your clothes? Look at the lilies and how they grow. They don't work or make their clothing, yet Solomon in all his glory was not dressed as beautifully as they are" (Matthew 6:28–29).

The biggest preparation we need to make while in this world is for what comes after—heaven or hell. Are you ready?

And for heaven, what you wear isn't important. It's come as you are.

Because in the long run, it's not what's hanging in your closet that the key—it's Who's holding your heart. It's not head knowledge; it's heart acknowledgement. Sometimes the longest distance is the 18 inches between your head and your heart.

Paul said in Romans 10:9–10, "For if you confess with your mouth that Jesus is Lord and believe in your heart that God raised him from the dead, you will be saved. For it is by believing in your heart that you are made right with God, and it is by confessing with your mouth that you are saved."

Have you done that? Have you said, "Jesus, come into my heart. I need You as my Lord and as my Savior"?

That's the key to "getting there." "For anyone who calls on the name of the Lord will be saved" (Roman 10:13).

Can you echo back, "Yes I'm ready"? If not, let's talk.

✓ REALITY CHECK

Have you called upon the name of Jesus and asked Him to fill your heart with His indwelling presence? If not, re-read Romans 10:9–10 and do it now. That's your preparation for heaven. Don't want to read it or commit your life to Christ? That's preparation for hell.

⧗ PRAYER PAUSE

Father, fill my heart with Your Spirit. Help me to grow in my knowledge of You and apply that head knowledge to heart acknowledgement as I seek to serve You and Your people.

✱ FOOTNOTES

1. Words and Music by Larry Norman©1970 Beechwood Music Corp./J.C. Love Pub. Co.

FOGGY DAYS

The joke about the weather in the Pacific Northwest is "if you don't like the weather we're having, wait five minutes"—sun one minute, rain, snow, or hail the next. Wait for it!

I say this because recently I was sitting in a hotel room in Newport, Oregon, which had a gorgeous view of the Pacific Ocean. The day before, I had spoken at a women's event two hours to the south. I knew I'd be exhausted when the event was over, and the thought of the five-hour drive home made me tired just thinking about it. So I booked a room in Newport, located on highway 101 along the Oregon Coast. I was right. The two-hour drive was all I could handle and with 30 miles to go, I prayed, "Please get me there!"

The sunset that night was awe inspiring. Nothing quite like seeing the sun silently slip into the ocean. As the sun set, the entire horizon, as far as my eyes could see, exploded into a brilliant red color. Gradually the brilliance faded as night fell, but the memory is etched in my mind. Loved this weather!

The next morning when I opened the curtains, the seagulls were squawking, and somewhere in the distance I could hear a seal barking. The sky was blue, the ocean waves white and I knew I had to get out and walk on the beach...in a bit. Did I mention I loved this weather?

Before I ventured out to get sand in my shoes, I had a memorial message to write for my friend Marie, who before she passed away, requested that I speak at her service. The purpose of the two extra nights at the coast was to pray, think, pray, write, and pray. I was locked away in my room, with the "do not disturb" on the door. I was in search of uninterrupted quiet time to gather my thoughts and summarize 40 years' worth of friendship into a 20-minute eulogy. Where to begin?

All morning I worked on outlining the message, praying my thoughts would honor Marie and my Jesus—her Jesus. I typed and typed, hit the save function (I've learned my lesson) and shut down the computer. The beach was calling my name. Oh yeah, love this weather! When I looked out the window, the sky was no longer blue. I could no longer see the ocean from my window. The fog had rolled in, obscuring the vision of my afternoon plans and destination—the beach. So much for the best laid plans for the day. This was *not* the weather I was waiting for!

As I wrote my message for Marie, I thought about where she is today and my earlier prayer while driving, "Please get me there!" Well, Marie is now there—where we all hope is our final destination—heaven. She's there because she placed her trust in Jesus. She prayed, "Jesus, I want to live for You. Please get me there." She didn't just go to church and fill a pew on Sunday. She didn't just take a seat at Bible study or load her plate at a potluck. She served the Lord without fanfare. Matthew 6:3–4 says, "Don't tell your left hand what your right hand is doing. Give your gifts in secret, and your Father, who knows all secrets, will reward you."

The reward for serving and following Jesus is not measured by worldly standards. It's not given to those who pursue it for recognition and reward. It's not given to those who spend a lot of time just "doing" but rather to those who spend time "being." It's given to the humble servant, who puts others' needs before their own. That was Marie. She learned, she lived, and she loved...and was loved. The reward she had been quietly pursuing, was now hers.

The fog never did lift that day. I missed my window of opportunity to walk on the beach. But I didn't miss my opportunity to spend time with the Lord. My best laid plans turned into God's best laid plans for me.

James 4:14–15 says, "How do you know what will happen tomorrow? For your life is like the morning fog—it's here a little while, then it's gone. What you ought to say is, 'If the Lord wants us to, we will live and do this or that.'" The weather was great when I arrived and then the fog rolled in. I ended up doing exactly what the Lord wanted me to do—rest, write, pray, and spend time with Him.

I learned a valuable lesson from my friend Marie—after her death. Life is short. Laugh often, love without ceasing, and don't take life so seriously. We don't know how many days we have on this earth. The fog rolls in and the fog rolls out, but sometimes the fog is of our own making. God is still there. He's still in control. And each day we need to live for Him.

"For I know the plans I have for you,'" says the Lord. 'They are plans for good and not for disaster, to give you a future and a hope'" (Jeremiah 29:11).

✓ REALITY CHECK

Is your vision foggy? Is it clouded by the things in life that are weighing heavily on your heart and mind? Take them to Jesus for a clear perspective.

⧗ PRAYER PAUSE

Father, there are days when I feel so paralyzed by the fog in my life that I can barely function. Jesus, help me release the control of my burdens to You. I know when I do, the fog will lift.

Dedicated to the memory of my friend Marie Rice,
Co-conspirator and sister in Christ. We had fun!
October 6, 1951 – April 30, 2009

IN THE STILLNESS

Not long ago, I found myself sitting on a rock along the banks of Hood Canal, journaling my thoughts. I'm not very good at journaling since my mind races faster than my fingers can keep up. But this day, I was writing. My mind and fingers were in sync. I was sitting and listening and waiting.

As I closed my eyes, I heard the sound of the waves hitting the shore. The seagulls were calling to each other as they skimmed the calm waters of the canal. Birds of all kinds were chirping. I wondered if they could understand each other's specific chirps. A fly buzzed my head. The wind blew through the trees that overhang the bank—trees that provided a shelter for me as I sat. A pinecone dropped silently in front of me.

I don't often sit still, but on this day I was listening to the sound of God's creation and my spirit was at rest. "Be still, and know that I am God" (Psalm 46:10 NIV).

Overhead, an airplane broke the sound of nature. On the road behind me, a car drove over the speed bumps, making a thump-thump noise. Then a logging truck released its very loud compression "Jake" brake as it took the corner and headed down the hill. What I heard behind me was the world. What I saw in front of me, was God.

"Search me, O God, and know my heart; test me and know my anxious thoughts" (Psalm 139:23 NIV).

I was sitting there, asking that God would do just that—search me. As I sat taking in God's creation and marvelous handiwork, I hoped heaven looked like this. No streets lined with gold for me. Just give me blue sky, green trees, and a body of water. *This* is paradise on earth.

There is something about water that soothes my soul. Perhaps this is why Jesus said we needed living water...water only He could provide...water that cleanses and renews.

To the woman at the well, Jesus said, "But the water I give them takes away thirst altogether. It becomes a perpetual spring within them, giving them eternal life" (John 4:14).

And her response? "Give it to me! I want it!" (John 4:15, my paraphrase)

I'm screaming..."I want it, too!"

I'd been at the canal for three days when I ventured down to the rock. And there, the Rock awaited me. Psalm 40:1–3 says, "I waited patiently for the LORD to help me, and he turned to me and heard my cry. He lifted me out of the pit of despair, out of the mud and the mire. He set my feet on solid ground and steadied me as I walked along. He has given me a new song to sing, a hymn of praise to our God."

Truth is, it wasn't me who was waiting patiently. (Patience and waiting are not my gifts.) It was God who was waiting patiently for me.

God spoke to Elijah saying, "'Go out and stand before me on the mountain,' the LORD told him. And as Elijah stood there, the LORD passed by, and a mighty windstorm hit the mountain. It was such a terrible blast that the rocks were torn loose, but the LORD was not in the wind. After the wind there was an earthquake, but the LORD was not in the earthquake. And after the earthquake there was a fire, but the LORD was not in the fire. And after the fire there was the sound of a gentle whisper" (1 Kings 19:11–12).

Are you in need of some quiet time with God? Find a rock, sit down, and be still. Ask God to shut out the world and listen for His gentle whisper.

"I wait quietly before God, for my hope is in him. He alone is my rock and my salvation, my fortress where I will not be shaken. My salvation and my honor come from God alone. He is my refuge, a rock where no enemy can reach me" (Psalm 62:5–7).

The Rock is waiting for you. Sit down, be still, listen, and wait... patiently.

✓ REALITY CHECK

Take a seat. He's waiting.

⧗ PRAYER PAUSE

Slow me down, Lord. Help me to focus on Your still, small voice that speaks to me in the quietness.

CONFLICT

I'm smack dab in the middle of yet another conflict, and I hate conflict. I didn't ask for it, but it found me. Seems it always does.

Oh, I'm not in any *big* conflict with any one person; I'm in conflict with myself. Truth is, this conflict has been my shadow since I was a toddler.

You see, I don't know if I'm right-handed or left-handed. I write left-handed and I throw a baseball right-handed. Eating? Bring it on! I can go either way.

If the right side of the brain controls someone being left-handed, and the left side of the brain controls being right-handed, what controls my brain? (I can hear you now...what brain?) Am I in my right mind or has my mind been left behind? (Again...no comments!)

There is a quirky test on the internet—which *must* be accurate because it's on the internet—that shows which side of the brain controls a person. The test features a dancing lady. Most people see the lady spinning counter-clockwise. They use the left side of their brain. Thing is, I see her spinning both ways...she is making me dizzy! I look at the list of right-left brain characteristics and I can fall under either side—or not. Can you see why I'm so conflicted here? Left side says

I'm detail-oriented. True. But it also lists math and science on that side, which is *so* not true of me. Right side brain functions is far more me... big picture, risk-taker, and imagination (which is very vivid) rules.

Conflict is nothing new in the world. Abraham and Sarah were the founders of conflict. Abraham had to be in conflict with himself when his wife Sarah told him to sleep with her maid, so they could have what they thought would be the promised child. That inner conflict exploded into an outer conflict with Ishmael, the maid Hagar's son and Isaac, Sarah's son. It's a conflict that continues today between their descendants. In spite of their innie and outie conflicts, Abraham and Sarah are listed in Hebrews 11's "great hall of faith." There *is* hope!

Our conflicted selves have one foot in heaven and one foot in hell, and most of us are dangling somewhere in between in this life on earth. Which world has the strongest hold on us? What the world has to offer, or what Jesus has to offer? I fear most of the times, it's the world that has the strongest pull.

Romans 12:2 reminds us, "Do not conform any longer to the pattern of this world, but be transformed by the renewing of your mind. Then you will be able to test and approve what God's will is—his good, pleasing and perfect will" (NIV). We are told that we are to be *in* this world, but not *of* this world.

Which is dominant in your life? The world's ways or God's ways? Temporary or eternal? "For this world is not our home; we are looking forward to our city in heaven, which is yet to come" (Hebrews 13:14).

David, a man after God's own heart, had conflict in his life. Boy howdy! If you read through the psalms, you will find him up one minute and down the next. Wonder which side of the brain he was controlled by?

Listen to David's words in Psalm 39:1-5. "I said to myself, 'I will watch what I do and not sin in what I say. I will curb my tongue when the ungodly are around me.' But as I stood there in silence—not even speaking of good things—the turmoil within me grew to the bursting point. My thoughts grew hot within me and began to burn, igniting a fire of words: 'Lord, remind me how brief my time on earth will be. Remind me that my days are numbered, and that my life is fleeing away. My life is no longer than the width of my hand. An entire lifetime is just a moment to you; human existence is but a breath.'"

Interlude

Notice at the end of his self-conflict and his war within...he rested. He got his ranting and raving out if his system and stopped. He rested, just maybe long enough to give it all to God. Seems that once we get into rant-and-rave mode, we're rock'n and roll'n with no end in sight. Pause, rest, interlude, selah.

It doesn't matter which way you see the lady dancing—whether you are left brain controlled, or right brain controlled. What matters is if you are God-controlled. He will use whichever side of the brain you work out of, for His good, for His glory...if you let Him.

Peace, the absence of conflict, to you all.

✓ REALITY CHECK

Do you have conflict in your life? Is it time to just "give it a rest"? Do it, now! Place your life in God's hands.

⧖ PRAYER PAUSE

Jesus, I give the conflict in my life to You. Help me release the need to be in control and have everything my way. Keep my heart and mind directed on what You know is best for me, not what the world thinks is best. Change me from the inside out, according to Your ways. Don't allow the world to change me from the outside in.

CHANGES

Every day, I drive past the familiar brick house on my way into town. Every day, I glance over at the house and remember the many hours I spent in the house and on the surrounding property.

And then one day it happened. I knew it would, but I wasn't quite prepared for what I saw. Next to the familiar oversized blue mailbox was a dreaded "for sale" sign. My childhood home overlooking the Lewis River was for sale. Well, it wasn't really *my* childhood home, rather my childhood friend's home. I spent many an hour playing at the neighbor's house, which was located across the street, through the ditch, over the barbed-wire fence, and down the ravine.

Roger, the neighbor boy and I spent many hours in competition: horse, pig, ping-pong, darts, Monopoly, and even the card game Flinch. We kept a chart with a tally of our win-loss record. We built forts, played on the old steam engines, and sledded down the steep hills in the winter. As little kids, we played with plastic army figures in and around the cornstalks in his mom's garden. He had no problem playing games with a girl...and my competitive nature wanted to beat him, a boy, at all activities! When Roger, all of his siblings, and the neighborhood kids graduated from high school and moved away, it was *then* that the parents built a swimming pool. Who said parents aren't smart?

Roger's parents passed away a few years ago and it was time for the house to be sold. Knowing that Clyde and Millie's house would be occupied by a stranger gave my heart a lurch. In my mind, the house will always be the Schurman House. We tend to name houses in this town: Miller House, Hoffman House, Stuart House, and the old Cheever Place. The original owners haven't lived there in years, but the names still stand. A newcomer to town can take up residence in the house, but *their* name will never be associated with it.

In 1963, Bob Dylan wrote and sang about change in his classic folk song with the lyrics, "The Times They Are A-Changin'." Whether we like it or not, change is coming. Every day offers change. We can embrace it or deny it, resist it or reject it—but it is going to happen.

There is only one constant in our life—one thing that never changes, and that is Jesus Christ and His love for us. "Jesus Christ is the same yesterday, today, and forever" (Hebrews 13:8).

Neighborhood landscapes change—houses are built, houses are torn down. Trees are planted and years later cut down. Fire and wind can destroy them all in minutes. But nothing can take away the memories. And nothing can take away the love of God.

"For I am convinced that neither death nor life, neither angels nor demons, neither the present nor the future, nor any powers, neither height nor depth, nor anything else in all creation, will be able to separate us from the love of God that is in Christ Jesus our Lord" (Romans 8:38–39 NIV).

In the days when Jesus walked the earth, He promoted change, and the people were frightened. It was all happening too fast. Who was this man? How could He claim to be God? And those very people who were anticipating His coming—who should have embraced Him—spit on Him and hung Him on a cross.

The message was radical. John the Baptist said, "Turn from your sins and turn to God..." (Matthew 3:2). *Sins? What sins?*

Jesus repeated that message in Matthew 4:17. *The Message* puts it this way, "Change your life. God's kingdom is here." *Surely He wasn't talking about me. Must be her!*

The childhood house will soon be occupied by someone new. I'll have to get used to that and let it go. Let someone else build their memories in that house.

The only house we need to focus on is the house where God resides—inside of us. We might have to make some changes to do that. We might have to clean house (argh) and toss some old things out. Old ideas, old hurts, and the old "I've always done it that way before" mentality.

As my friend Carol says, "I don't like to clean house, but I like a clean house." No pain, no gain.

If you've not made that change in your life—the change to *fully* embrace all He has for you—I suggest you start cleaning house now. Embrace Jesus and the love He has for you. And as you do...live it out loud!

✓ REALITY CHECK

Time to clean house? Out with the old, in with the new? Just remember, you still have your memories. Change can't take those away.

⧗ PRAYER PAUSE

Thank You, Jesus, that no matter how much the world changes around me, You never change. You are the same yesterday, today, and tomorrow. Forever! And You will never leave me.

FRIDAY NIGHT LIGHTS!

A few years ago, the Woodland High School class of 1969 had its 40th reunion. Believe it or not, that was the year I graduated from high school. Where *did* the years go?

Our reunion weekend started with Friday Night Lights...football! I hadn't been to a high school football game in years.

I walked around the track, which surrounded the football field, looking for a familiar face. Would I recognize former classmates? Would they look the same? As I walked, my ears were assaulted with the filthy language of the kids playing and running around while the game was in progress. Where were their parents? Surely I was never that bad?

The next night was our formal get-together. The years melted away and I was back to being called Barby...the nickname I grew up with. When I walked in the door, a man came up to me and said, "You look good! *Really* good!"

I had no idea who he was, but his words sure gave my ego a boost. I quickly looked down at his name tag. (Ah, that's who that was.) "How are you! You look good, too." (Not *really* good, but good.)

It was wonderful to reunite with classmates I hadn't seen in years. Many of them I went to school with all 12 years, many were in my youth group, including my *old* friend, Alice. I have known Alice longer than anyone else in my class since she was born two days after me in the same hospital. (And she always lets me know she's younger!)

As the evening progressed, I could see that over the years, I'd become a bit more reserved than some of my former classmates. Nothing wrong with good old fun...a bit of karaoke "at the Y.M.C.A" complete with arm motions was a riot to watch. I wasn't about to get up and participate. I never was very demonstrative when it came to this sort of thing. I was always afraid I'd look foolish and someone would laugh at me.

What I observed that night was attitude and actions. It seemed that some of *us* had never grown up. I had hung up my partying hat at about the 25th reunion. Earlier reunions, I was one of the wild children, partying until the lounge closed; but no more. I no longer longed for a Bud or a Jack Daniels or beat a path to the bar. Water actually tastes pretty good and I've found that I can have a good time without boozing it up.

I suddenly felt out of place. And I felt a sense of sadness, knowing that the majority of those in that room didn't know what I know. They didn't know Jesus. They were lost...and I doubt they even knew it, let alone cared.

Somewhere in the last 40 years, I had made a radical change in my life. The change actually began in the ninth grade when Alice, whose locker was next to mine all through high school, told me about an upcoming ski retreat she was going on. I wanted to go! But there was a catch to going skiing...I had to attend Wednesday night Niners group. I owe a lot to Alice. She was the one who got me to check out youth group. She invited, I declined. She invited, I declined, until finally I said yes. And on a snow-covered mountain, I found Jesus. Maybe I should say He found me, since I was the one who was lost. Someone else told me about Jesus that weekend and after a difficult struggle with myself, with my pride, with the fear of letting go, I invited Him into my life. I said yes!

As I think about Alice and the youth group, I'm reminded of the words of Paul in 1 Corinthians 3:5–7. "Who is Apollos, and who is Paul?...

Why, we're only servants. Through us God caused you to believe. Each of us did the work the Lord gave us. My job was to plant the seed in your hearts, and Apollos watered it, but it was God, not me, who made it grow. The ones who do the planting or watering aren't important, but God is important because he is the one who makes the seed grow."

Some people are called to plant seed of faith—to do the inviting to youth group; others are called to water—to nurture and encourage. We all play on the same team and can build on what the other has done. We all have our jobs to do, but as the scripture says, it doesn't matter who does which job. What's important is that God is the one who makes our faith grow. It is teamwork and the only one who gets the glory—the points on the board—is God.

As I think of where I was, where I am, and where I'm going, I think about this: I've been asked how many people I've led to Christ. It sounds like they're asking how many notches I have on my belt. It's a question I won't answer. It's not important to me. What is important is that I keep planting seeds and that I keep encouraging people to grow in their faith. Notches on a belt aren't important to me. Being faithful is. I'm not very good at keeping score. I lose count...but I love playing the game!

We have to remember that a flower won't bloom until someone has done the hard work. Till the soil, plant the seed, water it, and watch God make it grow. It's only then that we can see the flower bloom. Plant the seeds...keep tossing them out. Let God do the rest.

I've grown up over the last 40 years. First Corinthians 13:11–12 says, "When I was a child, I spoke and thought and reasoned as a child does. But when I grew up, I put away childish things. Now we see things imperfectly as in a poor mirror, but then we will see everything with perfect clarity. All that I know now is partial and incomplete, but then I will know everything completely, just as God now knows me now."

I don't have all the answers. But I do have Jesus. And while I'm still too intimidated to stand up and move to "Y.M.C.A" for fear I'll mess up,

I'm fear-less to stand up and wave my arms for J.E.S.U.S . I don't care if anyone laughs, or if anyone thinks I look foolish...because it's not about me.

Many of those classmates who attended the reunion were with me on that ski trip. Some are still serving the Lord; most are not. But I am hopeful knowing this: The seeds of faith in their lives were planted a time long ago. It took my seeds years to start to sprout. So there is hope. There is always hope.

✓ REALITY CHECK

Our hope is in the Lord. Let's sing and wave about Him!

⧗ PRAYER PAUSE

Father, there are people in my own family who don't walk with You. Help me to be a beacon of light that draws them to You. Help me to play my part as a Kingdom builder, whether that be planting or watering. And I pray You will reap a new harvest from their lives.

REAL POWER

I'm sitting inside the house, warm and snug at Hood Canal. It's rained every day since I've been here—and I do mean rained! The wind has been blowing so hard the rain seems to be coming down sideways. Last night, the power went out, and it could have been the biggest blessing of my time here.

My cell phone background light provided enough light to find a flashlight. The flashlight provided a path to the candles and the wood-stove. It was then I discovered a big problem: I couldn't find matches or a butane lighter to ignite either the candles or the stove. The container on the wall that usually held wooden matches was empty. Then I searched again.

It was during a second search that I found the lighter by the wood-stove.. It had been there all along, but it was hidden in the shadows.

Curling up on the downstairs couch, I began to read my Bible by candlelight and the glow of the fire coming through the glass door of the woodstove. I read about the woman who lost a coin and searched and searched for it. I thought about my search for a match. Neither of us gave up until we found what we were looking for. And what we were looking for was right under our noses.

I didn't sleep well last night. Actually, I didn't sleep at all. At 5:00 a.m. I was still wide awake. Maybe I've had too much sleep this week. I haven't done much on my "I want to be alone" personal retreat except sleep, eat, read, and write. Getting dressed was optional! It was wonderful!

Maybe I had too much tea to drink. Maybe it was the excitement of the evening events. Then again, maybe it was the inner struggle I'm having with myself—things that are heavy on my heart that kept me awake. Decisions I need to make and am avoiding. Decisions that haven't been made clear. Or perhaps they have been made clear, but I just don't want to face them and so keep putting them off. Perhaps it was God keeping me awake for a little conversation. As I lay on my bed looking up through the skylight, I cried out to God for direction.

Psalm 25:4–5 says, "Show me the path where I should walk, O LORD; point out the road for me to follow. Lead me by your truth and teach me, for you are the God who saves me. All day long I put my hope in you."

I cried out for guidance last night. And I asked that He would direct my path.

Verse 12 continues with, "Who are those who fear the LORD? He will show them the path they should choose."

I had to acknowledge and recognize who God is and that He knows better than I do about what is best for me...and for others. He is God Almighty, the Holy One, All-Knowing, and All-Powerful.

And I had to recognize who I was in light of who He is. I am weak, dependent, and in need of direction. He is God and I am not. I had to lean on Proverbs 3:5–6, "Trust in the LORD with all your heart; do not depend on your own understanding. Seek his will in all you do, and he will direct your paths."

I petitioned God to help me take one day at a time. Not to deal with the what-ifs of life, but with the "what is."

Philippians 4:6–7 reminds us, "Don't worry about anything; instead, pray about everything. Tell God what you need, and thank him for all he has done. If you do this, you will experience God's peace, which is far more wonderful than the human mind can understand. His peace will guard your hearts and minds as you live in Christ Jesus."

Peace is an inside job. My struggle was with myself. I was living in a war zone of my own making. Inner peace only comes when we recognize who we are. We are children of God. It's only when we take care of the innie, we can successfully become outties. We need to take care of internal issues before we can reach out externally.

Christ's peace lives inside of us. The Holy Spirit takes up residence, internally, and the evidence shows externally. Externally, the outside world can be in an upheaval. But inside, the peace of Christ rules.

"And let the peace that comes from Christ rule in your hearts" (Colossians 3:15).

I came to realize today that I am only responsible for my actions and re-actions, not those of others. I can disagree with how things are done—or not done—but it only creates conflict in my life. And it's our inner being where conflict resides. I need to remember that God is in control, not me.

The weather can change so fast up here. Pouring down rain and wind can quickly change to blue skies and gentle breezes. But don't blink; it can change back just as fast.

Last night when I went to bed, stars were shining through the skylight. This morning, I woke to the sun shining over the water. My last day here, and the Son had broken through.

I leave you with the words of Jesus who said, "I am leaving you with a gift—peace of mind and heart" (John 14:27). I just need to remember that a gift is useless unless it's unwrapped.

✓ **REALITY CHECK**

Are you struggling to find a sense of peace within? Look to Jesus. He is our peace. Let Him rule in your heart.

⧗ **PRAYER PAUSE**

Help me to remember not to worry about anything, instead to pray about everything. Father, I release the inner and outer conflicts in my life and exchange them for Your peace.

WALK IT OFF

I did something today I never should have done. I got on the bathroom scales. You don't have to say it, I know...big mistake. I thought my eyes weren't focusing. And then I looked again. Ouch! There was no mistake. I'd done it again—gained weight. What was even more frightening was I knew Christmas dinner was awaiting my presence at the table. Here I was, already past the danger zone.

It's amazing how easy it is to allow unwanted pounds to creep back on; a pound here and a pound there. Doesn't seem like a big deal, until one pound is added to another, is added to another. Soon all the determination and discipline it took to lose the weight has been wiped out. It's subtle you know, the gaining of weight. You think you have won the war of the weight when you realize you've only won a battle. And once you get comfortable and let up on the defense, the offense calories from the other side attacks.

Disgusted with myself, I tossed on a hooded sweatshirt, sweatpants, shoes, and mittens and started out the door. Oh yes, and my new Chris Tomlin CD blasting away in my ears. I walk, I worship. I walk, I sing along. I walk with arms outstretched and hands raised high. It's about me and God and what He thinks, not what passersby think.

As I walked, I thought about how—just like the weight creeping back on—sin creeps in. Gaining five pounds doesn't seem like a big deal, until five becomes ten and ten becomes fifteen. That good habit you worked so hard to follow—it's gone.

I haven't gone up in my clothing size, but emotionally I feel like I'm a loser, and I don't mean in pounds. Mentally I feel I've failed to keep up my part of the bargain, which was to keep the weight off.

It's the same with sin. How sly sin is, as one little sin becomes bigger until the sin becomes the new habit. Our willpower to fight the sin seems at times to be a losing battle.

We make this promise to follow and obey Jesus, and then we get sidetracked. A little here, a little there. We don't read our Bible one day, and one day becomes two and two becomes three. Talking with God is rare, except for maybe asking Him, "What else, God?" Church and regular fellowship become optional. Little by little it happens...and we wonder why we feel so disconnected from God. Who pulled the plug?

As I was doing my daily read-through-the-Bible program this week, it seems like the main theme each day is our sins. Great! (Just what I didn't want to read.) Galatians 5:19–21 lists a whole bunch of no-no's. They include sexual immorality, impure thoughts, eagerness for lustful pleasure, idolatry, participation in demonic activities, hostility, quarreling, jealousy, outbursts of anger, selfish ambition, divisions, the feelings that everyone is wrong except those in your own little group, envy, drunkenness, wild parties, and other kinds of sins. To that list you can add murder, adultery, greed, stealing, lying, conceit, and homosexuality. (BTW, this is God's list, written in His book. I didn't make it up.)

Our demise all started with a *want*, accompanied by the deception that surely one fruit wouldn't hurt. And one became two and two became three...and one cookie led to another. And hey, let's give all our friends cookies too. One bad apple or cookie *can* spoil the whole bunch.

With the cookie, the thing is that people can tell if I've had too many by my appearance. On the other hand, many of those sins listed in Galatians can't be seen with the naked eye; they can only be seen by God. And God looks at the inside of a person, not his appearance. First Samuel 16:7 says, "People judge by outward appearance, but the Lord looks at a person's thoughts and intentions." Don't get me wrong, people will indeed be able to see those sins in your life. They will come out through your actions and attitudes.

Sometimes I'm more concerned about how I look and about what others think than I am about what God thinks. I pay more attention to how others view me and less about how God views me. And that is just "stinkin' thinkin'."

First Corinthians 10:13 tell us that "the temptations that come into your life are no different from what others experience. And God is faithful. He will keep the temptation from becoming so strong that you can't stand up against it. When you are tempted, he will show you a way out so that you will not give in to it."

You mean even when tempted with cookies, pie, and ice cream? Yes, I believe so!

What I need to remember is simply (or not) to stay away from such indulgences—away from the bakery section and ice cream freezers. I need to learn to hang out with the fruit and maybe, just maybe, spiritual fruit will be produced in my life. The fruit Galatians 5:22–23 calls, love, joy, peace, patience, kindness, goodness, faithfulness, gentleness, and self-control.

Second Timothy 2:22 says we are to *run* when tempted! "Run from anything that stimulates youthful lust. Follow anything that makes you want to do right. Pursue faith and love and peace, and enjoy the companionship of those who call on the Lord with pure hearts." So when I walk into the grocery store and I smell the cookies...*run!* Head to the produce section...tear into an orange!

I need to walk to keep my weight off and my blood pressure down. Healthy eating isn't enough.

Being in the Word daily helps to keep my spiritual life up and my sinful nature down. And I need to be in fellowship with others, pray without ceasing, and constantly work on my relationship with Christ.

So get on your walking shoes and walk the path with me. Let's not be so much concerned about how we *look* to others, but pay attention to how we look to God. While it's important to be healthy and eat correctly, let's focus on what is on the inside—our spiritual health. Walk with me through the Bible this year and around the track. It's the healthy thing to do.

✓ REALITY CHECK

Push back from the table, put down the cookie, and lace up your shoes. Praise God for His presence in your life and walk that sin right out of your life.

⧗ PRAYER PAUSE

Jesus, I look to you. "Oh, the joys of those who do not follow the advice of the wicked, or stand around with sinners, or join with scoffers. But they delight in doing everything the LORD wants; day and night they think about his law" (Psalm 1:1–2).

ARISE SHINE

I don't *do* early mornings, if I don't have to. That said, I consider anything before 10:00 a.m. (on my day off) early. So when I was invited to speak at an early-morning women's Christmas breakfast I groaned, smiled, and accepted. That meant I had to not only get out of bed on a Saturday, but get dressed.

"Arise, shine, for your light has come,
and the glory of the LORD rises upon you" (Isaiah 60:1 NIV).

You will never see me bounce out of bed when the alarm clock makes that obnoxious noise...unless I've overslept. I don't have a "good morning, Lord" attitude until *at least* the second cup of coffee. Eyes are usually blurry, mind is foggy, and my body rebels when my feet hit the floor. Rubbing my eyes only makes my vision worse. Where are my glasses? Thankfully, I haven't lost the sense of touch! Ah, there they are! I see more clearly with contact lenses since my glasses are sadly in need of a new prescription. No way could I get contact lenses in my eyes first thing in the morning. And with each year I fail to get new glasses, my vision fades.

So on a freezing December morning, after exchanging glasses for contacts, and two cups of hot black antifreeze in me (aka coffee), I headed out the door. Surprise! Our driveway was a sheet of ice and our street wasn't much better. Gratefully, the freeway was clear, thanks to the cars of early morning travelers thawing the road.

There was a thick layer of fog hanging low to the ground, which made for limited visibility and slow driving. At the top of the first hill, the sun appeared through the hazy fog. Ah, clear driving. Time to step on it!

I realized that the sun is always there; sometimes it's just hidden behind fog or clouds. And the sun does not move...we do. The earth revolves around the sun, not the other way around. It never changes. And neither does God. He is always there, even when we think we can't see or sense Him. Hebrews 13:8 says, "Jesus Christ is the same yesterday, today, and forever." I don't know about you, but in a changing world, I find that so reassuring. Even when I don't sense His presence, He's there.

The fog lifts, the rain stops, the snow melts—eventually. The sun will shine through.

First Corinthians 13:12 reminds us, "We don't yet see things clearly. We're squinting in a fog, peering through a mist. But it won't be long before the weather clears and the sun shines bright! We'll see it all then, see it all as clearly as God sees us, knowing him directly just as he knows us!" (MSG).

We'll see God as clearly as He sees us, when we open our eyes...when we open our minds...but most importantly, when we open our hearts.

He is not just looking down on us; He is surrounding us. Open your eyes, look around, get up, and get going. Your alarm clock is waking you up with:

"Arise, shine, for your light has come,
and the glory of the LORD rises upon you" (Isaiah 60:1 NIV).

Oh, and getting up early to share God's Word is a joy, an honor, and a privilege.

✓ REALITY CHECK

Do you struggle to see God through the fog of the world? Arise shine! God's light is shining on you. Open your eyes. The fog will clear.

⧗ PRAYER PAUSE

Father, on those days when I just want to pull the covers over my head and hide, "Open my eyes to see the wonderful truths in your law" (Psalm 119:18). Wake me up, Lord!

GREAT EXPECTATIONS

Am I amazed or am I in awe? That is the question. Truth is that I'm a bit of both. If amazed means surprised, then the answer is no! However, I am filled with an overwhelming sense of wonder and in total awe, or respect at what my Jesus is able to do, if only I ask. I know God can and will do whatever He wants, whenever He wants, however He wants, and with whomever He wants. Sometimes, He even wants what I want, and when I want it (which is usually, *now!*).

Recently, I sent out a huge mass mailing to "random" churches for the speaking ministry God has entrusted to me. Let me tell you how in shock and awe I was when the *next* day I received a response from one of the churches. The very next day! And another call the day after that! The postal cancellation ink on the envelope was barely dry. The mailman must have just delivered the mail only minutes before I received that first call. Ta-da! Bull's-eye. Two days, two bookings, one referral and one "let's talk."

It all began with prayer. I went before the Lord with, "Lord, what churches should I mail my information to?" I hit the "Google" app button and began the long and tiring research of looking up addresses of churches. I prayed as I addressed, stuffed, licked, stamped, walked to the post office, and mailed the envelopes. I prayed that the info would land on fertile soil. I prayed for the person who would receive the information and prayed they would be able to use me for His glory. I prayed, as the material went out. Over three hundred envelopes were tossed into the U.S. (and Canadian) postal service. Would any of them take root? (Would they even arrive?)

Jesus tells us about someone else who randomly did the same thing, only instead of envelopes, he send out seeds.

In Matthew 13, Jesus talks about a farmer who went out to plant seeds. The farmer tossed them all around. Some landed on a path and became food for the birds. Some fell on ground full of rocks, and the roots couldn't dig in, so they died. Some ended up with the thorns that eventually choked the life out of the good plants as they both grew. However, some fell on good, fertile soil and produced a huge crop—way more than had even been planted. (My paraphrase). The farmer planted, and then left the results to God.

What have I learned? Plant seeds because God tells you to—not for a reward. But also plant expectantly. He is looking for obedient people who will do His will, people who aren't looking for credit, glory or applause for themselves, but who will give it all back to the One who sent them out in the first place.

I believe God can and will use any of us, if we are willing. I believe faith has to be active, not passive, and we physically have to move when He calls and be in action for Him. Our faith in Jesus Christ demands a response from us. A response to act, not just sit. How would a church know I had a speaking ministry if someone didn't tell them? And how will people know about Jesus if we don't share our faith. Faith—not works, not religion, not rules, not regulations—faith.

How many of those envelopes will take root? Only God knows. So far, eight have been returned due to incorrect addresses. Of those, three I was able to re-send. No, I don't quit easily.

Two churches have officially invited me to speak at events where non-Christians will be in attendance. I am praying that even now, the soil is being prepared, and I'm excited to think about how many people could be reached through one envelope landing on someone's desk.

James 5:16 tells us, "The earnest prayer of a righteous person has great power and produces wonderful results." Prayers = great power = wonderful results. Pray with great expectation that God not only hears, but He acts.

Each one of us has a ministry. "He creates each of us by Christ Jesus to join him in the work he does, the good work he has gotten ready for us to do, work we had better be doing" (Ephesians 2:10 MSG). God is opening doors for you to serve Him. Will you walk through them?

And remember this: It all begins with prayer and more prayer and more prayer. James 4:2–3 says, "The reason you don't have what you want is that you don't ask God for it. And even when you do ask, you don't get it because your whole motive is wrong—you want only what will give you pleasure."

So, Jesus, I wait expectantly for what You are about to do. (And I thank You for what You have done and are doing.) Will I be amazed at the result? Yes, because Your love *is* amazing. Will I be in awe? Oh yeah! And I stand in awe of You, Jesus!

✓ REALITY CHECK

You have a ministry! Haven't figured out what that is? Pray and ask Jesus to open doors for ministry opportunities. When He does, walk through them.

⧗ PRAYER PAUSE

Father, help me to discover the gifts and talents You have given only to me and then to use them for Your good, for Your glory.

☐ FOR THE RECORD

I love the story of the reluctant leader—Moses. Reluctant, yet he was obedient to God. And God moved when the people moved. The Red Sea parted when the people walked toward it. Not until. Can you imagine what they must have been thinking? First, that they were trapped. Army coming up behind them, water in front. And then to see the sea divide and provide an amazing escape route. They weren't walking on water, they were walking through it. Waves on each side, dry land under their feet. What a sight that must have been.

Miracles happen! Pray! Wait for God to move mountains, or part seas.

OUCH!

It was a fun-filled weekend at the annual retreat of a wonderful group of ladies from a Nazarene church in Oregon. The weather cooperated with blue skies, warm weather (a novelty for the Pacific Northwest in February), and even warmer hearts. And once again—great food, which was, once again, plentiful!

On the way home, I stopped at a Starbucks and had coffee with a friend I hadn't seen in some time. Great conversation, and of course, great coffee!

When I got home, I pulled the car into the garage and began to unload the boxes that couldn't wait until morning. It was then that it happened. I slammed the car door, forgetting my thumb was still hanging onto the door.

There are no words to say what I was feeling. As a matter of fact, I *said* no words. I can honestly say Ephesians 4:29, "Do not let any unwholesome talk come out of your mouths, but only what is helpful for building others up according to their needs, that it may benefit those who listen" (NIV), was working for me. All my energy and thoughts were focused on how much pain I was in. Even my little toe was aching, sympathizing with the rest of my body. That one thumb put my world on hold.

I was feeling what David must have meant when he said, "I am suffering and in pain. Rescue me, O God, by your saving power" (Psalm 69:29).

I made it up the steps and into the house. From the other room, my husband said hello, and I managed somehow, to answer back. At the sink, I tried to run cold water over my thumb. The water only increased the pain. I'm surprised my head wasn't bruised or aching from banging it on the counter as I spoke the only language I knew...groans!

The next day, my thumb began to turn dark shades of blues, purples, and reds. I thought about painting all my fingernails to match, but we all know what it looks like when I paint my own nails. (Not a pretty sight!) Now my thumb, did indeed, *stick out like a sore thumb.*

It's amazing how we take something like a thumb for granted, how we don't even realize we use it all the time, until it's smashed and throbbing.

Matt Redman sings, "Blessed be Your name on the road marked with suffering." [1] Oh man, was I suffering. I might not have been blessing His name...but at least I wasn't doing what Job's wife suggested and cursing God.

I know I will lose the thumbnail. I can see the old nail is working its way upward, as a new nail is trying to push through. (And yes, I've been picking at it!) The new nail is not visible to my eye right now, but I know it's there. Psalm 23:4 says, "Even when I walk through the dark valley of death, I will not be afraid, for you are close beside me." Sometimes when we're walking through the valley, we forget it's *through* and we will come out on the other side. We also forget that Jesus walks the path with us.

Romans 5:3–4 encourages us with, "We can rejoice, too, when we run into problems and trials, for we know that they are good for us—they help us learn to endure. And endurance develops strength of character in us, and character strengthens our confident expectation of salvation." While I certainly didn't feel like rejoicing or praising God as my thumb throbbed, I can tell you I'm developing the painful endurance of a long-distance runner. I know there is a finish line ahead, healing at the end.

Wounds often leave scars, yet an old American proverb says, "Time heals all wounds." Pain and hurt will heal, with time. It's what we do during that waiting time that will make or break us.

Peter said, "In his kindness God called you to share in his eternal glory by means of Jesus Christ. After you have suffered a little while, he will restore, support, and strengthen you, and he will place you on a firm foundation" (1 Peter 5:10).

No matter what happens in life—dashed dreams, disappointments, loss, or a smashed thumb—He will see us through to the other side, if we let Him. He restores, He supports, He strengthens. And as that process is taking place in my life, my feet stand firm on the Solid Rock of Jesus Christ. How about yours?

✓ REALITY CHECK

How firm is your foundation?

⧗ PRAYER PAUSE

Jesus, through hardships and pain, joy and laughter, You are there. Strengthen my character so that I might praise You, even as I experience life's difficulties. Help me to remember to praise You in the good times, and praise You in the not-so-good times.

✱ FOOTNOTES

1. Matt and Beth Redman. ©2002 Thankyou Music

ALL IS READY

With the threat of snow the other night, I kept sneaking peeks out my patio curtains. I was keeping an eye on the weather conditions with the anticipation of a school kid hoping that school might be cancelled. There was no snow, only frozen molehills...and something else looking back at me. I'm used to seeing squirrels in our backyard, but not rabbits.

Okay, so what do rabbits eat? Duh! Carrots! I went to the fridge and pulled out a carrot, cutting it up in small pieces for the rabbit and tossed it out on the patio. *Four* days later, the carrot was still there. As Elmer Fudd would say, "Stupid wabbit!"

When the snow finally arrived and the temperatures dropped well below freezing, I noticed no birds were flying around in search of food, or sitting on our fence. I rummaged through the garage, quickly finding the birdseed. Bundling up, I went outside and spread some around the patio, on the bench, and planters. And I waited. No birds!

I thought, what is wrong with you birds? I've left food! Come and get it! Do you want to starve?

This morning, as the birds finally found the food, I was hit with yet another "bump into God!" reminder. My Jesus was saying, "I have placed food in front of you and you ignore it. You are starving and you still ignore Me." Ouch!

The birds were looking in the frozen yard for food and there it was, right in front of them. They didn't even have to work for it; they just had to eat! The table was prepared before them!

"Jesus said, 'I assure you, Moses didn't give them bread from heaven. My Father did. And now He offers you the true bread from heaven. The true bread of God is the one who comes down from heaven and gives life to the world.'

"'Sir,' they said, 'give us that bread every day of our lives.'

"Jesus replied, 'I am the bread of life. No one who comes to me will ever be hungry again. Those who believe in me will never thirst'" (John 6:32–35).

Are you hungry? Are you thirsty? Are you tired? Stop struggling on your own. The hand of our Savior is reaching out to you. Grab it!

All is ready. The table is set. Eat.

✓ REALITY CHECK

Open your eyes and see what is right in front of you. Jesus has prepared the table. Stop searching for meaning, for life, for acceptance, for love somewhere else.

⧗ PRAYER PAUSE

Father, give me that bread of life, that living water that can only be found in You. It seems I waste so much time looking for love from outside sources, when You are living inside of me. Thank You for being a hands-on, up-close, and personal God.

▯ FOR THE RECORD

The birds have eaten all the seed I threw out for them and have come back for more. They know where the hand is that feeds them.

FREEDOM!

It was quite a week. Jesus rode into town on a donkey, as the crowd of people shouted "Hosanna" (save us) all the while waving palm branches as they celebrated His arrival. The people thought He had finally accepted His role as king. Yet it was not the kind of king they expected. A week of celebration was just beginning.

The celebration was for Passover. There was one last meal on Thursday with friends in an upper room. Friends He knew and loved denied Him and sold Him out for personal gain. Those people who called themselves religious leaders sought ways to get rid of Him. He challenged their rules and traditions. They didn't like it. He preached God, not rules. There was the kiss in the Garden. Seriously, a kiss? He was hauled away for a mock trial. The people were given a choice, Him or a murderer. One would be released. The religious leaders incited the riot, yelling, "Give us Barabbas!" Seriously? What must Barabbas have thought? A guilty man being released; an innocent man taking his place. Oh, if he only knew!

The gutless ruler left it up to the people what to do with this man. "Crucify Him!" they shouted. Seriously? Those people who had praised Him a few days earlier, who were His friends, now turned and betrayed Him.

Beaten, disrobed, and forced to carry His own method of death, a cross, Friday was a difficult day. Soldiers nailed Him to the cross between two men who had been sentenced to die. One mocked Him as he knew death was imminent. The other changed his attitude and said, "Remember me." The Man in the middle replied, "You are going with Me" (Luke 23:42–43, my paraphrase).

As the thunder rolled, the temple cracked, and He took His last breath. His friends took His body and laid it in a tomb. And that was that.

Saturday was a quiet day. It was over, or so they thought. The end of the story? Not even close.

Sunday morning was just another day, until the women went to the tomb, found the stone that blocked the entrance had been rolled to the side. Looking inside the tomb, they saw no body. Their friend was gone, in more ways than one.

It took a while, but the light finally came on. He was exactly who He had said He was. He had indeed risen from the dead. Why should that have surprised His followers? He had brought people back to life right in front of them. Maybe they had been skeptical those three years they walked with Him. Maybe this was what really convinced them. (Me, I would have been convinced with the water-to-wine trick.)

But without Friday, there is no Sunday.

As I look at this story, so familiar to many of us, I think about my own life. Those I walked with for years betrayed me. People I bumped into at the grocery store—people who ran with that crowd—turned and walked the other way when they saw me. I had been told to leave, but not told why. Hung out to dry because the religious leaders didn't like my presence. I questioned; I challenged. I wanted more of Jesus, not more fluff and stuff. That was a Friday. Saturday was calm. And Sunday came. And with Sunday, freedom!

I share this with you as a reflection. We've all walked the path Jesus did in one way or another. He rose above it and so can we. And when we do, there is freedom. No more bondage to rules and traditions. "So Christ has truly set us free. Now make sure that you stay free, and don't get tied up again in slavery to the law" (Galatians 5:1).

Sometimes the best and hardest thing we can do is to walk away. Being told to leave is hurtful; yet it also served a purpose, a plan. The chains were removed. I no longer had to behave and worship according to people's expectations, rules. "We've always done it this way before" was behind me. The chains were gone. I was free! "Now the Lord is the Spirit, and where the Spirit of the Lord is, there is freedom." (2 Corinthians 3:17 NIV).

Because Jesus paid it all, we are free. Free from bondage to sin. Free from the "we've always done it that way" mentality. We are free to serve Him, with all of our "heart, soul, mind and strength," according to Mark 12:30.

If you're in a church that does not preach the Word of God, but the word of the world, you need to be set free. John 8:32 says, "You will know the truth, and the truth will set you free." The Truth is sooooo refreshing. The Truth is Jesus.

✓ REALITY CHECK

Do you know the Truth? Do you know Jesus?

⧖ PRAYER PAUSE

Jesus, You are the way, the truth, and the life. Help me to follow Your way, live Your truth, and enjoy the life You have given me.

WORSHIPPING AND WAVING

My mom and I drove 140 miles north to Seattle one summer to attend two weekend worship services, held out-of-doors, on back-to-back, perfect Northwest afternoons. (Perfect in the Northwest means it did *not* rain!) There is nothing like worshipping with 40,000 plus, like-minded people.

We arrived at the stadium early both days, just to soak up the charged surroundings. Food was being served around the event venue, while the staff busied themselves with last-minute preparations for worship. Key personnel who would be featured during this 2½-hour worship service were making their own warm-up preparations. Worshippers began to fill the seats and you could hear the excitement building. An *anthem* was sung about a banner waving, followed by the opening prayer—"Let's play ball!"

As the worship service began, people were clapping their hands, raising their arms, or standing and yelling words of encouragement like "you can do it" or "way to go!" You can't help but get caught up in the "wave." We sang a hymn about the history of our worship called, "Take Me Out to the Ballgame." Everyone knew the words by heart. That *hymn* transitioned into the next *hymn*, the unofficial song of Washington State. If you are a baby boomer, you know something about a guy named Louie and that he and his friends had to "go"...yeah, yeah, yeah, yeah. Nice people with heavy trays came through the seats offering us drinks (for a huge donation).

Can you tell I was pumped? How I wish Seattle wasn't over two hours away or I'd be worshipping there more often!

By now you have probably figured out that I wasn't at church. No, I *worshipped* that weekend at Safeco Field, home of the—you guessed it—Seattle Mariners baseball team, my idols! The staff that was making the preparations was, of course, the "dancing groundskeepers," and those warming up were not the praise team, but the object of my praise and adoration—the baseball players!

Our team won both games we attended, so there was much clapping and standing...and, of course, the "wave." In case you've been under a rock, the wave is when the people in the stadium stand up, one stadium section at a time, with arms in the air, while yelling something unintelligible like, "wheeeeeeeeee!" It creates a wave effect all around the stadium. Seattle fans are professional "wavers" as the wave began at the University of Washington, just up the road from the stadium, many years ago.

It's frightening, actually, when I think about what God thinks of me worshipping something or someone other than Him. In Exodus 20:3, He said, "Do not worship any other gods besides me," followed by, "don't make idols of any kind—don't bow down to them—I am a jealous God." (See Exodus 20:4–5.)

Romans 1:23 says, "And instead of worshipping the glorious, ever-living God, they worshipped idols made to look like mere people, or birds and animals and snakes."

My idols didn't just look like mere people, they *were* mere people! I was worshipping what God had made, instead of God Himself.

I get excited about going to a baseball game (which I skipped church to attend) and the opportunity to see my heroes in real-life, instead of just on TV.

As I thought about this "worship" experience, I thought about my "real" worship service, held on Sunday mornings. How excited do I get when Bible study night rolls around, or early morning Sunday school? Did I even bother to read the chapter we are about to discuss in class? What about Sunday worship service? Have I even checked once to make sure I have my Bible in the car before I leave the house? Or has it been in the backseat since *last* Sunday? What I did put in the backseat and on the backburner, was God.

There is nothing wrong with taking a Sunday off from church to go camping, fishing, or even to a baseball game, as long as you don't make a habit of it, or for that matter, make these activities an idol. If doing these things excites you more than spending time with God, beware. God said He is a jealous god.

What is your idol? Your children or grandchildren, money, work, vacation home, a boat, or a car? Fill in your idol ____. Your idol is whatever takes your focus off God. Whatever you put before Him. You don't plan it, it just happens. Pretty soon, you've built your own altar, with a golden cow or a bronze baseball bat. No runs, no hits, no errors, and God is not left on base.

Now to be honest, I don't really worship the Seattle Mariners—honest! I will admit, however, that I do have a passion (or addiction) for baseball. And give me some credit here, I did obey one of the Commandments that weekend. That would be #5, "Honor your father and *mother*." My mom might disagree on that one, since I wore her out, dragging her all over Seattle. Mom, you're a good "worshipper"—I mean "sport!"

✓ REALITY CHECK

Who or what is your idol? Your priority? Remember: God first, family, job. Don't let the world tell you otherwise.

⧗ PRAYER PAUSE

Dear Jesus, sometimes I forget to put You at the head of my life. Even in ministry, I fail to follow Your lead. Help me to keep You first in my life and to remember that all blessing flow from You.

THE EARLY ARRIVAL

The phone rang in the middle of the night, scaring me out of a deep sleep. I hate those calls as my first thought is that someone died. Usually it's a drunk asking for Susie or Mary, or whoever.

It was hard to recognize the voice at the other end of the line. I couldn't tell if he was laughing or crying. The voice was that of my son, Matt. He said they were at the hospital and his wife Joann was going to have the baby—their first and our first grandchild—and she was going to have it *now*. He was not laughing.

What Matt was saying didn't make sense. Clara was not due to arrive for at least another seven and a half weeks. This was an emergency! The baby needed to be delivered by emergency C-section immediately.

I shot out of bed, told my husband what was going on. I threw on some clothes and shot out the door, leaving my husband—who was still in bed—behind.

The 20-minute drive to the hospital took 15. How I drove through the tears that were flowing was beyond me. I prayed and cried all the way. Tears of joy and tears of desperation, pleading with God that both mama and baby would be okay.

"LORD, hear my prayer! Listen to my plea! Don't turn away from me in my time of distress. Bend down your ear and answer me quickly when I call to you" (Psalm 102:1–2).

Soon after I arrived, our 2-pound, 15-ounce Clara emerged at 1:30 a.m. She was tiny, but a fighter. The nurse took my camera and snapped pictures of our oh-so-small, little girl.

I listened as the nurse explained the situation to daddy and the maternal grandparents. I'm not sure it even penetrated my brain. I felt such fear that our little baby was too small to survive, not to mention the health of her mother.

We couldn't see either Clara or her mama during those wee hours of the morning. Only the daddy could. I stepped up and said, "Joann's mama needs to see her daughter! Let her poke her head in her room to be reassured she's okay!" They did. (Don't mess with mamas, ya hear!)

I went home to try to get some sleep. My shell-shocked husband asked why I didn't wait for him. I told him he was too slow!

The next day, we went back to the hospital. There was our little baby, lying in an open incubator, a basinet-type baby bed, sound asleep. We couldn't touch her, only look. I continued to pray, to plead with God to let this little life continue to breathe. The only tube connected to her was for feeding, as even eating expended energy. This was why we couldn't touch her early on, as touch stimulates the body, and she needed all the calories she could get. She was breathing on her own; this was good. Neonatal intensive care was her home, and her mama and daddy's for the next month or so.

As we stood watch over our sleeping granddaughter, God heard my prayers, my cries in the night and during the day.

Psalm 121:1–2 says, "I look up to the mountains—does my help come from there? My help comes from the LORD, who made the heavens and the earth!"

As I prayed over our granddaughter, I continued to pray from Psalm 121, "The LORD himself watches over you! The LORD stands beside you as your protective shade" (v. 5).

This was four years ago. Today our little Clara is a bright, beautiful, blonde-haired, blue-eyed four-year-old. She is also the big sister of equally adorable two-year-old Renee. God's blessings have been poured upon us. It's such a gift to see these little girls with their wonderful daddy, my little boy. Psalm 127:3 tells us, "Children are a gift from the LORD."

We dedicated Clara's daddy to the Lord many years ago, asking that He teach me how to be a good mom, and to raise Matt up in the faith. My son is a gift from God, on loan to me. The night Clara was born, I entrusted her into God's hands. She is Yours, God.

"The prayer of a righteous man is powerful and effective" (James 5:16 NIV). I don't know how righteous I am, but listen up, great things happen when a believing person prays. Try it; then watch and wait.

✓ REALITY CHECK

Sometimes when we pray, we don't know what to say other than "help!" And you know what? It's good enough. Romans 8:26, "And the Holy Spirit helps us in our distress. For we don't even know what we should pray for, nor how we should pray. But the Holy Spirit prays for us with groanings that cannot be expressed in words."

⧗ PRAYER PAUSE

Prayer should be our first thought, not our last resort. "I look to the mountains—does my help come from there? My help comes from the LORD, who made the heavens and the earth!" (Psalm 121:1-2).

⧉ FOR THE RECORD

Matt, this little boy we dedicated to the Lord, is now the pastor of Camas Friends Church, Camas, Washington, and pursuing his PhD in Christian Spirituality.

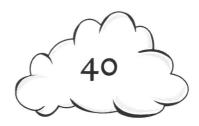

40

COME OUT, COME OUT

"**W**ait for it!" I tell myself this every time I drive the stretch of Interstate 5, just south of Olympia, Washington. Trees and bushes grow on each side of the freeway, green in spring and beautiful reds, oranges, and yellows in the fall. When I drive north or south, coming or going, I look to the left, then to the right, waiting. When I see what I'm looking for, my heart does a little flip-flop. There it is, or they are, in all their majesty—deer.

It's not a totally uncommon sight in this state to see deer along the road as "roadkill," after a run-in with a car, but to actually see them grazing along the grassy area near the trees is a sight to behold. It seems like it is only on this stretch of the freeway that they make an appearance for me. Sometimes one, sometimes the whole family, is out for a stroll and lunch. I wait, I see, and move on, satisfied that I have seen these beautiful creatures. As I approach the area where I usually see the deer, the anticipation grows. I begin singing out loud (or to myself if I have a passenger) the words of a song based on Psalm 42, "As the deer pants for streams of water, so I long for you, O God."

I feel as though God has shown Himself to me through these deer. There are days when the deer do not appear. It's disappointing, but I sing on, and wait...for next time.

The deer emerge from their hiding place among the roadside trees in search for food and water. It's a brave move on their part. You never know what might be waiting as they timidly come out of the forest and into the open area. A car? A hunter?

Sometimes we are like those deer. We too hide, emerging from our hiding places in the forest or the haze or our own making, seeking food...seeking God. Our bodies hunger and thirst. So do our souls. Food for the body is temporary, but the living water from Jesus satisfies the hunger in our souls.

When I was a kid growing up in Woodland, Washington, there were two pipes coming out of the hillside at the bottom of Green Mountain Road. Water poured from the pipes continuously. I was never sure where the water actually came from. I only knew that the water was clean, cold, and refreshing. It was a rest stop for me every time I rode my bicycle by it. Stopping my bike and getting off was risky since there wasn't much room on the side of the road, and logging trucks whizzed by regularly. But oh, it was worth it! The pipes are still there, but the water is no longer running. Seems like a sign of the times.

Our souls thirst for living water; yet for one reason or another, we think we can quench that thirst by turning on the water tap. (Or for some of you, opening a bottle of water.)

Jesus said to the Samaritan woman at the well in John 4:10, "If you only knew the gift God has for you and who I am, you would ask me, and I would give you living water."

In John 7:37–38, Jesus stood and shouted to the crowds, "If you are thirsty, come to me! If you believe in me, come and drink! For the Scriptures declare that rivers of living water will flow out from within."

The Spirit of God, the Living Water, is available to all who put their trust in Him. Drink. Be satisfied. Never thirst again. Don't wait. Come out of your hiding place in the woods. Eat, and drink all the God has for you. Pursue Him! He's waiting.

Chapter three of Habakkuk touches my soul. Habakkuk's prayer painted a pretty dismal picture of crops failing and animals dying. No figs, no grapes, no cattle in the stalls, and flocks dying. Yet in spite of his circumstances, Habakkuk was able to say, "I will rejoice in the LORD! I will be joyful in the God of my salvation! The Sovereign LORD is my strength!" Then he caps it off with, "He will make me as surefooted as a deer, and bring me safely over the mountains" (v. 18–19).

God gives us strength to get through life's difficulties. Keep your eyes focused on God.

In my dreams, I imagine myself jumping and running like a deer! (Only in my dreams!)

Be alert! Wait and watch! Don't miss all that God has for you.

✓ REALITY CHECK

What are you expectantly waiting for? Focus. Wait.
He is worth it!

⧖ PRAYER PAUSE

Father, as I go through life, help me to keep my eyes focused on You. On days when I don't feel You near, remind me that no matter what is going on in my life, You are indeed right beside me. "Rejoice in the Lord always. I will say it again: Rejoice!" (Philippians 4:4 NIV).

LET IT GO

Leaving a church is difficult, under any circumstances—difficult good, or difficult bad. When I left the church I grew up in and worked at— difficult didn't even come close to describing it. Much of my life was centered on that church and its people. Suddenly, it was gone.

God had been making my situation extremely difficult. I no longer felt the joy of serving Him in that environment. God was calling me out, but I was hanging on. The longer I stayed, the worse it got. When the words finally came, "Your services are no longer need" I was in shock. I'm not sure why. The committee just got through to me where God couldn't.

Driving away one last time, it only took three blocks to feel the load lifted. I suddenly felt free. By the time I reached the second stop sign, the words of scripture were loud and clear, "No one can serve two masters. For you will hate one and love the other, or be devoted to one and despise the other. You cannot serve both God and money" (Matthew 6:24). I was afraid to leave the job because of the paycheck. And God reminded me that He would take care of me and all of my needs (Philippians 4:19).

For a long time, the enemy worked on my mind. I questioned what I had done since no answers were given to me. I felt betrayed by those people I called friends...people I trusted. I thought my people skills were in the toilet and quite frankly, I felt like I sucked as a person. I stopped writing, feeling I had nothing positive to say.

I'm sure Joseph felt the same way after he was sold into slavery by his brothers, only to rise to be Pharaoh's right-hand man. Years later, his brothers went to Pharaoh for help because of a famine in their land. Who is there to greet them? The brother they'd sold. Joseph says to them, "God turned into good what you meant for evil" (Genesis 50:20). Yes! That is what I felt!

Jesus must have felt the pain of betrayal by those closest to him... those He trusted. And being God in the flesh, He knew who, what, when, where, why and how this would happen.

Painful memories still linger after more than six years. I remember, but those memories don't consume me. People avoided me in the store. I felt shunned. Those who did speak said, "I heard..." and what they said was totally inaccurate. Others who walked the other way when seeing me the grocery store, will now speak to me. Of course, I speak first. Take the offensive, right? I'm letting it go, letting it be. The past is the past. God knows. I know. Good enough!

What have I learned? Listen to God! If He is moving you to a new place, go when He calls. God has used this difficult period in my life to further His kingdom. I'm sure of it. When I let go of one page, new chapters were right behind. My prayer is always that I will get out of the way, so God can have His way.

I've been reminded that people are not God! We are all imperfect creatures, sometimes we hurt and sometimes we help.

God has opened new doors, just as He promised, and I've learned to walk through them—the first time He asks. God has restored my writing. He has led me to a church where the Word of God is preached boldly. My hurts have healed. He does that.

✓ REALITY CHECK

Have you been hurt by the church? Give it to God. Ask Him to heal the wounds inflicted by His imperfect people. You are no longer in bondage to their painful arrows.

⧗ PRAYER PAUSE

Jesus, help me to forgive those who have wounded my soul. Help me to move past the hold these hurts have on my life. When I come face to face with those people who inflicted the pain, help me to smile, say hello, and move on.

PAST, PRESENT, FUTURE

Let me set the scene. I was at work. It was a Friday and I had forgotten to make next week's work schedule for the one hundred telephone operators in my office. Even worse, I had forgotten to turn in the payroll. I had plans for the evening and the weekend—plans I could not cancel. One hundred furious telephone operators were about to skin me alive.

Then, I woke up! I tried to go back to sleep, but this dream (or nightmare) was so vivid that I couldn't shake it. Where was my worksheet, the operators' requests for days off, the file to show their work shift preference? Why wouldn't people leave me alone to look?

People often ask me why I have never written stories about my telephone company years. After all, I was there for 19 years. Well, I guess my nightmare from last night about sums it up!

Truth is, those were my wild days. I wasn't sure how I could fit God into a story—until now.

I started working for Pacific Northwest Bell in Portland, Oregon, when I was 20. There wasn't much to do in a big town, for a small-town girl, especially when I didn't know anyone. A few months later I turned 21. By that time, I had gotten to know my coworkers. Now I was "legal," single, and living in my own apartment. Get the picture?

I hated living in the big city with all the traffic lights and the constant sound of sirens from emergency vehicles. I was alone and lonely in the midst of people. After a couple of years, I moved back to my hometown and commuted 30 miles each way to and from work, five days a week, for the next 17 years. Seems my party days were just beginning. During the phone company years, I married and had a child, and the partying slowed down.

I became a youth leader at my church to middle school-aged kids, grew in my faith, attended Sunday school and Bible studies, and was at church every time the door opened. No, I did not join the choir. That was a blessing to everyone.

I accepted Christ as my Lord and Savior when I a teenager. When I left home for college, I left God at home. The party scene was fun! Yes, I had accepted Jesus, but it seems I wasn't very good at following Him. Accepting Jesus into your head is one thing. Allowing Him access to your heart is another.

Oh, I know He was with me. There was no doubt about it. I just ignored Him. As I look back over the years, I see how He pursued me, relentlessly, through the good, the bad, and the ugly. I share this with you to let you know that God can use anyone, regardless of your wilderness years.

Look at the people in the Bible: God used the old, the young, the widowed, the murderers, the adulterers, and the prostitutes. And you think He can't use you? Seriously?

One of my favorite verses in the Bible that I cling to is 2 Corinthians 5:17: "Those who become Christians become new persons. They are not the same anymore, for the old life is gone. A new life has begun!" Outwardly we look the same, but on the inside we have been re-created.

It's always fun to run into people from my "past" at the post office or grocery store. When asked what I'm doing these days, you should see their faces when I say, "Well, I worked at a church, I've written two books on seeing God, and I speak at Christian women's retreats all across the country." Their jaws usually drop and their tongues become tied. Pretty amusing actually.

If God can use and speak through a donkey, He can use me. He can use you. (Read Numbers chapter 22.)

The past is the past. Leave it there. You don't live there anymore. Move on!

Philippians 3:13–14 reminds us: "I am focusing all my energies on this one thing: Forgetting the past and looking forward to what lies ahead, I strain to reach the end of the race and receive the prize for which God, through Christ Jesus, is calling us up to heaven."

Won't you consider Him? Look at me! See what God has done! Your story, like mine, could make a difference in someone else's life. Share it. Make a difference. As the words to the old song say, "Amazing Grace, how sweet the sound, that saved a wretch like me. I once was lost, but now am found. Was blind, but now I see." [1]

✓ REALITY CHECK

Are there things in your life that you feel disqualify you to serve God? That is simply "stinkin' thinkin'." God can and will use you, no matter what you've done in your past. Give Him your past, your present, and your future. Then stand back and watch Him work in and through you in the here and now.

⧗ PRAYER PAUSE

Thank You, Jesus, for loving me so much, for taking this wretched person that I was and giving me new eyes to see and a new heart to serve You. Give me boldness to share the transforming power of Jesus and the work You are doing in my life with others.

✱ FOOTNOTES

1. John Newton. Amazing Grace. Public Domain

AUTOMATIC

There are many things in life that come automatically to us; we do them without thinking. Take breathing, blinking our eyes, or pardon me, peeing. Or in my case, eating! The one thing that doesn't come automatically to me is driving an automatic transmission car. I've never owned one, until now. The change has not be easy, not... automatic. I've never owned a car with P, R, N, D on the shift lever. It's always been an "H" formation with "1, 2, 3, later 4 and finally 5, plus R." There have always been three pedals on the floor, instead of two.

So why the change? Cuteness! I always judge a car by its looks! Oh I drove the car with the "H" and then compared it to the P, D, and R car. Without a doubt, the PRND car was zippier than the 1-2-3-4-5 car. (I'm all about zippy!) A small SUV with a stick was not the same as a Mazda 3 with a stick. I had every intention of continuing my stick-shift style, but drove away as an older, mature adult.

The first time I was stuck in Portland stop-and-go traffic, I was singing the praises of no clutch!

My friend Carol, who drives an automatic (mini-van mind you), told me driving a manual transmission vehicle was a control issue for me. She might be right, but so? I loved the action of shifting gears! The good news is that the new car has a manual option with "paddles" to shift down and then back up. Not quite the same, but still fun.

The problem is...I'm still reaching for the clutch and having a hard time remembering to put the car into park before trying to pull the keys out of the ignition. I pull up to a stop sign and automatically reach for the clutch and the stick. I guess I'm just a creature of habit.

Thinking about my "control issues," I am reminded how out of control my life is, without God. I need to constantly remind myself that *He* is in control.

God is *not* my "co-pilot" as I've seen on so many bumper stickers. He is *the* pilot. We don't share the driving duties. As much as I hate being the passenger (control issues again), with God I'm in the passenger seat, He is the driver, for the entire trip of my lifetime.

In Matthew 4:17, as Jesus began His preaching ministry, He said, "Turn from your sins and turn to God, because the Kingdom of Heaven is near." Turn away from a life of self-centeredness and self-control and turn to Jesus. Let Him guide your path, give you direction, and take the control.

Paul reminds us in Romans 6:6–7: "Our old sinful selves were crucified with Christ so that sin might lose its power in our lives. We are no longer slaves to sin. For when we died with Christ, we were set free from the power of sin." It's not about the power we have. It's about the power Christ has. He is in control. He has set us free from the power, from the control, from the hold that sin has on our lives.

We need to submit to His authority. Release the reins of control, relax in the passenger seat. Let God do the driving. Our job is to let Him! Such freedom awaits when we do. It's not automatic on our part. It takes constant work—and just like my need for the clutch will someday disappear, so will the need for control, as we place our trust and our lives in Jesus Christ.

✓ REALITY CHECK

If you need someone in a clutch, He's your guy. Start now. Eternal life doesn't begin when you get to heaven; it begins on earth the second you admit your need for a Savior, confess your sins, and ask Jesus to take control!

⧗ PRAYER PAUSE

Jesus, I release control of my need to be in control to You. Be my guide as I maneuver through life. Help me to follow You and not try to lead. Your way is the right way.

NEWS FLASH!

News flash! I am not perfect. Here's another news flash; neither are you! None of us are.

I've always found it interesting to hear how non-Christians believe Christians should act. Interesting, yet sad.

Over the years, I've had one person fill the role of the proverbial "thorn in my side." Any opportunity to make a "dig" at me was taken. For years I've let it roll off my back. There was one time when he was making fun of me and I responded, very calmly, with, "That really hurts my feelings." He came unglued, calling me all sorts of nasty names. I did not respond.

More recently, he was ranting about something and I calmly said—many times during the rant—that I was not responsible for what he was talking about. When I say I was talking calmly, I mean very calmly! He immediately was shaking his fist at me, screaming, "You call yourself a Christian?" He then unwrapped each finger, one by one, and proceeded to list what I did not do, things this non-believer thought I should do as a Christian. I can't tell you what attribute each finger represented. My ears closed at the first finger. It was as if God was protecting me from the vile outbreak of anger. When the fingers had been counted off, my hearing was restored and he said, "You are such a hypocrite!"

This tirade all came about because I was speaking calmly and not arguing. I simply stated a fact: "I am not the one you need to speak with."

I'm not sure what this person thinks the attributes of a Christian are—since he is not one.

What does a Christian look like? On the outside, we are vastly different. On the inside, we don't all respond to life's circumstances in the same manner. That said, our standard is found in Galatians 5:22–23: "But when the Holy Spirit controls our lives, he will produce this kind of fruit in us: love, joy, peace, patience, kindness, goodness, faithfulness, gentleness, and self-control."

That's the ideal, yet even though the Holy Spirit resides in me, I fall so short. Let's face it, we all fall short. "For all have sinned; all fall short of God's glorious standard" (Romans 3:23).

I don't even know what started the rampage directed at me. He was mad; I was talking calmly. I was fighting fire with water, not fire with fire. I'm not a shouter. You pick a fight with me, my voice will switch into calm mode, shifting down a gear. People who know me well, know that when I drop my voice, beware. It seemed to make this aggressor even madder, as he kicked his tirade up a level.

Here is what I've learned: Don't take the tirade personally though it hurts and leaves us wounded. He was trying to provoke me and was rejecting everything I stand for. And in doing so, he was rejecting Jesus.

I've started praying for that person. He doesn't know the great "I Am," nor does he know I'm praying. Chances are if he did, his response would be "don't bother!" I bother, not because I want to, but because I'm commanded to. When someone starts in on you because you're a Christian, scripture says to pray for them! Seriously? But I don't want to!

Romans 12:14: "If people persecute you because you are a Christian, don't curse them; pray that God will bless them."

God will bless them? Hardly seems fair, does it? Yet even Jesus prayed for His persecutors while hanging on the cross. Quite the example, don't you think?

Remember this, the Gospel is offensive to those who are perishing. "If the Good News we preach is veiled from anyone, it is a sign that they are perishing. Satan, the god of this evil world, has blinded the minds of those who don't believe, so they are unable to see the glorious light of the Good News that is shining upon them. They don't understand the message we preach about the glory of Christ, who is the exact likeness of God. We don't go around preaching about ourselves; we preach Christ Jesus, the Lord" (2 Corinthians 4:3-5).

The light in us, the reflection of Christ, acts like a mirror and exposes their sin. Light exposes darkness. When people know what we stand for, and Who we stand with, that can set them off without our even uttering a word. Sad, but true.

I encourage you to stand up for what is right. You might get knocked down again, but get back up. And honestly, in some cases, we just need to shake the dust off of our sandals and walk away. But continue to pray!

Peter said if we are to suffer, suffer for Christ. "This suffering is all part of what God has called you to. Christ who suffered for you, is your example. Follow in his steps" (1 Peter 2:21).

Something else to consider: We are just the messenger. We didn't make up the material. God did. So when I hear via the grapevine, "Well Barb says..." It's not my message I bring, but His. Don't shoot the messenger.

✓ REALITY CHECK

Stand for what is right. Be a light in a dark world.

⧗ PRAYER PAUSE

"He who began a good work in you will carry it on to the completion until the day of Christ Jesus" (Philippians 1:6 NIV).

Father, help me stand firm in my faith and remember that tirades directed at me are really not about me at all, but about the person delivering the hate-filled speech. May they come to know the true Deliverer.

GRANDMA'S HANDS

One of the things I remember about my maternal grandma was her hands. It wasn't the size or length, or whether or not they were perfectly manicured that I remembered. It wasn't that she used them to bake cookies, can pickles, sew (ick) or wrap meat at the local grocery store. It was the brown spots on her hands. She called them "age spots." Makes sense to me since she was, after all, old. (I thought they were freckles.) It seems that my grandma had been old for a very long time, or at least in this child's mind she was.

I always thought it odd that my "old" grandma was such a fan of sports. She was always at the high school games, shouting at the refs and cheering on the team (in that order).

What is even odder, as I look back, is that when she was rooting the team on, she was younger than I am now. Sigh.

Naturally it surprised me when I developed a "freckle" on my hand, then another, and another. Not to be left out, a freckle appeared on my temple. I was certain they were not old-age spots. After all, I'm not old!

I didn't want to think of myself as middle-aged, especially when that AARP invitation arrived in my mailbox. I should have accepted the middle-age title when I had the chance; now I'm asked, "Senior discount?" Just yesterday at the fast-food drive thru, I was asked, "You aren't 60 yet, right?" Bless her heart! The good news is, discounts!

My grandma was my age when she passed away...way too young!

And now, I'm a grandma. I don't "think" old, but there are days when I "feel" my age. My mind thinks I can still play shortstop, diving for the ball, and firing it to first. I'm also under the delusion that I can still smash a homerun and speed around the bases. My back and knees tell me a different story.

What I have noticed the most about growing older, is how I'm treated. If one more person calls me "ma'am," "sweetie," "dearie," or "hon," they might just find out how good I was with a baseball bat.

My vision—how I see the world—has not changed. How people see me has. If I crack a joke with the young person at the checkout stand, they just look at me with a "yes ma'am." I feel that I'm being ignored by my little part of the world. I see me as young; the mirror tells me another story.

I'm reminded of a woman who was sitting next to me in a Sunday school class many years ago. She made a comment about raising up young women in the church, teaching them, guiding them, getting them involved. Her next comment threw me: "But I'm just coasting now." I sat there for a minute, thinking should I or shouldn't I? And I did. I asked her, "How can I learn from you, if you're just coasting?" There was no answer, only dead silence in the class.

When we were saved, we were called into full-time service. There is no retirement in God's army. Psalm 92:14 says, "Even in old age, they will still produce fruit; they will remain vital and green."

I hold on to that verse as I grow older. No matter what our age might be, we are still useful to God, no matter what the world might think. We need to stop listening to the world and pay attention to the Word.

I pray that in my life, and in yours—no matter what your age—you will continue on the journey. You will never stop seeking God's face.

Hold on to the words of the Psalmist. Psalm 71:7–8 says, "My life is an example to many, because you have been my strength and protection. That is why I can never stop praising you; I declare your glory all day long."

My hands might be showing their age, but let me tell you this: I can still lift them to praise my God and King. Psalm 63:4 "I will honor you as long as I live, lifting up my hands to you in prayer."

"And now, in my old age, don't set me aside. Don't abandon me when my strength is failing" (Psalm 71:9). The good news is that He won't.

✓ REALITY CHECK

Don't pay attention to how the world sees you. Focus on how God sees you! You are His beloved treasure!

⧗ PRAYER PAUSE

Jesus, as long as I live, I will praise and worship You. You look at what is on the inside. You look for a heart turned to You.

DIZZY BLONDE

Go ahead, call me a dizzy blonde. I deserve the title, I've earned it—the hard way. Not often will you find me bouncing off the walls...not these days anyway. My "party-the-night-away" days are long behind me.

Yet, early one morning my alarm went off, reminding me to get up and check in online for my flight to Berkeley to see my granddaughters. The room was spinning and my body was bouncing off the walls as I made my way to my office. Somehow, I managed to get checked in (I wanted to be in Group A to board), then bounced my way back down the hall to bed.

Something was wrong with me, that much was clear. A stroke? A brain tumor? I became fast friends with the bathroom wastebasket, now taking up residence by my bedside. I finally gave in and told my husband, "Take me to ER." That in itself was frightening, as he hates to drive on the freeway, and I hate riding with him! He was scared. I was scared.

The hospital emergency waiting area is not a great place to be, especially when you're clinging to your friendly bathroom wastebasket. Checked in, wristband in place, and the wait continued. More information was needed, so I was whisked off to a cubicle, my "friend" still with me.

Finally, I was wheeled into an ER room. It was freezing! By now, my sister had arrived. "Ask them for a blanket!" I asked. Then, "Get another one!" I didn't know what was happening, but I knew there was no way I could get on an airplane the next morning.

Onward for a scan. I was asked if moving into a cylinder for the test would make me sick. Seriously? The CT showed my head was fine or at least fine, meaning no damage and nothing suspicious. Whew! I've had cancer, so a brain tumor was high in my thoughts of what could be wrong.

Diagnosis? Vertigo. It would eventually go away the doctor said. Eventually?

How about now! No, it would take time. Time? My sister called and cancelled my flight, along with our plans to spend Thanksgiving at the beach. (FYI: Those turkey TV dinners aren't bad.)

The hospital sent me home with a prescription for Valium and sea-sick pills. Seriously, seasick pills without taking my bucket-list cruise? Seems like I slept forever. I didn't want to move my head. I couldn't move it if I'd wanted to. My "friend" was still with me. I ended up losing five pounds that week. Not a great way to lose it, but effective. I didn't even attempt to drive a car for a week or two, as I couldn't look to the left or the right without my head spinning. A walker helped me walk down the hall, keeping my balance centered as I moved ever so cautiously. The walls were safe.

I should have seen this coming. Two days earlier on my way to church, I had looked to the right and felt like my head was spinning. It was like I was on a carnival ride, upside down. I brushed it off as too much coffee and not enough food that morning. Light-headed, right? What it was, was the beginning. And I ignored the warning sign.

I understand that with vertigo, a crystal or "rock" breaks loose in your ear, causing the imbalance. Yes, I officially have rocks in my head, to go along with the dizzy blonde status.

Amazing sometimes, how God gets our attention. I can hear Him saying, "I think I'll shake up the rocks in her head to keep her still for a while." He knows I'm not good at being still. (I'm good at being lazy, but not still.) This was a wake-up call for me. Slow down, girl. Your body might not move as fast as it once did, but the junk circulating in your mind (and your ear) is going at warp speed.

All kinds of thoughts attacked my mind. What if this happens again? What if I'm driving in traffic, on an airplane, speaking, or planning to speak? What if I'm alone? I had allowed the enemy to enter my thoughts.

And it all came back to one thing: God. I needed to remember that He is in control and He will not let me stumble. I needed to focus and fix my eyes on Him, "the author and perfecter of our [my] faith" (Hebrews 12:2 NIV). He might let me bounce into a few walls, but He will never let me stumble, if I keep my eyes on Him, remembering that He will never leave me alone. Deuteronomy 31:8: "Do not be afraid or discouraged, for the LORD is the one who goes before you. He will be with you; he will neither fail you nor forsake you."

God gives us warning signs. He told Lot's wife not to look back at Sodom and Gomorrah as they were fleeing the city or she would become a pillar of salt. She ignored the warning, taking a quick peek and immediately turned into a pillar of salt. God commanded Jonah to go to Nineveh. He ignored the warning. The crew of the ship Jonah was a passenger on tossed him overboard into the sea, where he was swallowed up by a big fish. Do you think someone smelled fishy when he emerged three days later? Both Lot's wife and Jonah suffered consequences; only one was able to redeem his actions.

On my way to church that Sunday morning, God sent me a warning sign. I ignored the warning. The good news is that He brought me, and other drivers on the road that morning, safely through it. I wasn't texting and driving; I was losing my marbles.

James 4:8 says, "Draw close to God, and God will draw close to you." Funny how something as "simple" as rocks in your head brings one into a closer relationship with the Father. It did me.

I'd like to say I depend on God 100% of the time. I can't. I still try to do things on my own, still run ahead of Him. James tell us, "When you bow down before the Lord and admit your dependence on him, he will lift you up and give you honor" (James 4:10).

Okay, God, I admit it and I bow down before You. Thank You for this rock-moving-in-my-ear experience. Thank you for reminding me that You are the Rock, and You never move.

✓ REALITY CHECK

James 1:12 says, "God blesses the people who patiently endure testing." How patient are you?

⧗ PRAYER PAUSE

Thank You, Jesus that You are the Friend who is always by my side. You have said in Your Word that You will never leave or abandon me. I hold on to those truths. (See Deuteronomy 31:6; Hebrews 13:5)

FOR FURTHER STUDY

Read Psalm 121. He's got you covered!

GIVE THANKS

Today is Monday and I'm not moving very fast. This is really nothing new for me, especially after a busy weekend. Two days ago, I participated in the American Cancer Society's Relay for Life. Each year, I walk 40 laps—that's ten miles—in memory of my college friend Marie who lost her valiant battle with pancreatic cancer.

So today, I ache. Today, I'm confident that I have muscles I didn't know I had before, or at least haven't used in a while. What I do feel is those dead bones come back to life!

Sixteen years ago, I was diagnosed with breast cancer. A lumpectomy and seven weeks of radiation later, and I'm still cancer free, alive and kicking (though legs don't kick very high).

Hearing the words, "You have cancer" was unexpected. I always schedule my mammogram every year and I never imagined anything would be wrong. I've shared my story in my first book; I won't go into detail here.

I've heard people say that when they received the diagnosis, "You have cancer," that they either began to pray or prayed more. These were people who didn't go to church, who knew about God, but not about Jesus. And this is where I have a question. Now that you have been healed, or are in remission, do you still pray? Or did you make that big plea to be healed, and once you were healed, went about your merry way? As a praying person, let me say that I prayed even more.

Maybe the prayers weren't for you, or for your health. Perhaps your prayers were for a job, finances, a wayward child, a spouse, a moving decision, or simply a cry for help. If your prayers were answered, in the way you hoped, did you continue to pray, giving thanks?

I prayed for strength. Strength to get through what I was about to go through. Strength to tell my family and friends. Strength for each day, as each day came.

When I came to the end of the tunnel of radiation and five years of drug therapy, I could have just said, "It is finished. Thanks God, see ya." But I didn't. God wouldn't let me. He asked me to share my story. I said, "Thanks, but no thanks." Well, you can see how far that answer got me.

Psalm 30:1 says, "I will praise you, LORD, for you have recused me. You refused to let my enemies triumph over me." The enemies of cancer, heartbreak, or disappointment.

Verse 2 continues with, "O LORD my God, I cried out to you for help, and you restored my health." Yes!

Here's the kicker in that psalm, found in the last verse: "I will give you thanks forever!" (v. 12).

Are you continuing to give Him thanks? Do you talk with Him daily? Trust me when I ask this that I'm talking to myself too.

Ephesians 5:20 tells us, "You will always give thanks for everything to God the Father in the name of our Lord Jesus Christ." Did you hear that? Give thanks for everything! When? Always!

Jesus tell us that we are more valuable than the sparrows. "So don't be afraid; you are more valuable to him than a whole flock of sparrows" (Matthew 10:31).

Now, here's the rub. Many people will desperately cry out to God in their time of need and call it good, even if they have no idea who God is, or Jesus. And that's the end of it. They ask, they are healed or get what they want, end of story. Consumer faith. Eat the food, fill your stomach, and go on with your life.

Jesus doesn't have a magic wand that He waves in your direction when you make a wish. He is not a fortune-telling machine that you drop a quarter into and receive an answer on a nice shiny token with, "Your wish has been granted." Jesus said, "I am the way, the truth, and the life. No one can come to the Father except through me" (John 14:6). The way to life is through Jesus. He's the bridge you need to cross, the bridge that leads to eternal life.

Bottom line: We need Jesus, all the time—not just when life throws us a curve. When we have Him in our lives, curveballs are much easier to hit or catch.

Remember this: "Keep on praying. No matter what happens, always be thankful, for this is God's will for you who belong to Christ Jesus" (1 Thessalonians 5:17–18). Paul is not saying to give thanks for everything that happens to us, but to be thankful that God is with us in the good and bad times.

Read that verse again. It says "you who belong to Jesus." Contrary to what TV advertisers tell you, or cultural or current thought might be, we are *not* all God's children. We were born in His image (Genesis 1:27). He loves what He created, but we are not automatically His children. Please understand this: "But to all who *believed* him and *accepted* him, he *gave the right* to become children of God" (John 1:12, italics mine.).

What did you say? How do you do this? I'm glad you asked: Confess your sin, admit your need for a savior, believe Jesus was born, died and rose again. And ask Him to take over the control center of your life. (Romans 10:9–10 paraphrase) Paul notes in Romans 8:14: "For all who are *led* by the Spirit of God *are* children of God" (italics mine).

Please, do this now. Eternal life, life with Jesus, begins on earth the second you surrender your life, and it extends beyond the grave into eternity. When you do this, there will be a party going on in heaven!

And remember, "Give thanks to the LORD, for he is good! His faithful love endures forever" (Psalm 136:1).

✓ REALITY CHECK

Read Psalm 136. Count how many times the verse says "give thanks."

⧗ PRAYER PAUSE

James 1:12: "God blesses the people who patiently endure testing." Help me to remember to praise You in the good times and to praise You in the not-so-good times.

For more information on the Relay for Life: www.relayforlife.org

SOAR!

It's the simple things in life that entertain me—things that usually don't require a ticket or reservations. Free is a very good price.

When I was a kid, my mom would drive my brother, sister, and me to an area on Marine Drive near the Portland, Oregon Airport. She'd pull the car off the road onto a wide area that served as a makeshift parking lot. There we waited and we watched as the massive airplanes took off and landed at PDX. It was free entertainment and I was awe-struck. "Look here comes another one!" I don't know the scientific explanation of how planes fly, and I wouldn't understand it if you explained it to me. When I buckle my seatbelt on an airplane, my prayer is always, "Lord, I don't know how these things stay in the air, I'm just thankful that they do. Please get us up and get us down safely."

I still love to watch the huge airplanes soar as they take off and burn rubber as they land. The sight of them just captivates me. Yet what I just described doesn't hold a candle to what I saw recently.

I was sitting in a chair on the deck at the Hood Canal house, gazing at the water and listening to the quiet, when I heard an unmistak-able noise—a loud scream. I looked up just in time to see a massive bald eagle fly directly over my head. Its wing span was huge. There was no time to take cover—or close my mouth! While the eagle was much smaller than an airplane, it was much more impressive. It...was... awesome! Wow! The bird landed in a nearby fir tree, and the branch bowed down under the eagle's weight. Perched high above the waters of Hood Canal, it sat, observing the comings and goings of the world.

My memories drifted back to July 20, 1969, when Neil Armstrong, the Apollo 11 astronaut, spoke the following words when he landed on the moon: "Tranquility base here. The eagle has landed."

My thoughts exactly! I thought of just how peaceful I was at that moment, sitting there doing nothing except *being*. Then the eagle landed. I've read that eagles have wingspans between 79–90 inches. And how do they fly? What keeps them up? Eagles rely on thermals. Thermals are rising currents of warm air and updrafts generated by terrain, such as valley edges or mountain slopes. That made sense...we were on the water, in the valley, with the Olympic Mountains to the west. Now that, I understood...sort of.

The eagle is so fierce-looking yet so majestic and awesome. There is nothing quite like them. I sat on the deck every day, waiting for one to fly by. (And I was not disappointed.)

As inspiring and uplifting as the sight of those eagles were, I was reminded that there is none like our God; nothing compares. The Creator is even more majestic and awesome than His creation.

Exodus 15:11 says, "Who else among the gods is like you, O LORD? Who is glorious in holiness like you—so awesome in splendor, performing such wonders?" There is none like You! Funny how those words, "glorious," "awesome" and "performing wonders" refer to God. Yet I tell you this: On that day the eagle flew over my head, it certainly described him.

"O LORD, our Lord, the majesty of your name fills the earth! Your glory is higher than the heavens" (Psalm 8:1). What an exclamation point to my time away and my God/eagle sightings!

Once again I had retreated to the canal to rest. God sent the eagle to remind me of Isaiah's words: "Even youths grow tired and weary, and young men stumble and fall; but those who hope in the Lord will renew their strength. They will soar on wings like eagles; they will run and not grow weary, they will walk and not be faint" (Isaiah 40:30–31 NIV).

Working for the Lord is easier on those days when we soar like eagles. We love those days when we are on a roll, running, walking...and not getting tired. But let's face it: When the day is done, everyone gets tired and needs sleep. So look to God, find your strength renewed. Whether you're a high-flyer or a low-rider, let God be the thermals that keep you going. Allow Him to lift you up and carry you through whatever assignment He has given you. Then, when you have no strength left, let Him be your strength. When you are about to quit, call upon the name of the Lord. He's awesome; He's majestic; and there is none like Him.

✓ REALITY CHECK

Are you tired and worn out trying to go through life on your own strength? Spread your wings and allow God to carry you. You will soar!

⧗ PRAYER PAUSE

Father God, I am in awe of You and Your creation. Thank You for lifting me up on eagles' wings and setting my feet on solid ground. You are my strength, my rock, my hope, and it's in You that I place my trust.

LOST AND FOUND

How many times do we talk about luck? I've heard, "Good luck; you'll do great" to "Good luck; you'll need it!" We've all heard about the "luck of the Irish." We have lucky numbers, lucky shirts, and a lucky rabbit's foot.

Friday was my lucky day. I parked my car and went into a store to pick up some things for my mom. We moved mom into assisted living a few months ago, so my sister and I have the job of making sure she has personal items in her apartment.

On my way back to my car, I noticed paper money wadded together on the pavement, just behind a car. Oh yes, my lucky day. I bent over and picked it up. All I could see was $20, but I knew there was more. Since I'm so honest, I walked around to the driver's side of the car where I had found the money to see if the driver had lost the money. In my mind, I could see someone opening the back end of the car, putting the groceries in the trunk, and then accidently dropping money. Had this been a coin, I would have kept it and continued on.

My husband finds money all the time when he walks. He tells me that men tend to wad up bills and put them in their pockets, along with their keys. Then when they dig in their pocket for keys, out comes the money.

No one was in the car! My lucky day! Finders keepers, loser weeper...

right? In ancient Rome, the term "finders keepers, loser weepers" meant that whoever finds something by chance is entitled to keep it. Mine! It was my lucky day indeed.

I got in my car and counted the money. Oh yes! Behind the $20 was another $20 and then $10. This was my lucky day. $50 was my prize for the day.

And then it hit me. My niece had dropped off money for me from the sale of stocking hats I had knitted and she had sold for my Relay for Life fundraiser. Guess how much she gave me? Yep, $50. The exact amount I had found.

I realized that I had put the money in my pocket, along with the list of things to pick up for my mom—and you guessed it, the money came out with the list. This was indeed my lucky day. No one had discovered my money while I was in the store. I had found my own money! Thing is, it wasn't really my money. I was giving it all away.

Matthew 16:25 says, "If you try to keep your life for yourself, you will lose it. But if you give up your life for me, you will find true life." Odd, isn't it? You have to lose something to find something.

We read about a rich young man in Matthew 19:16–30. He posed this question to Jesus: "Teacher, what good things must I do to have eternal life?"(v. 16). Jesus goes on to give the man a list of do's and don'ts...the Ten Commandments. The man must have let out a sigh of relief, as he checked off this "good-to-go" list and said he'd done those things. Then he asked if there was anything else. He should have stopped while he was ahead.

Jesus said to him, "Go and sell all you have and give the money to the poor, and you will have treasure in heaven. Then come, follow me" (v. 21). Scripture says the young man "went sadly away because he had many possessions" (v. 22). He loved his "stuff" more than he loved Jesus.

Would it have mattered that day if I had not found the money? I'm sure my car would have been thoroughly cleaned out as I searched for the missing money. That would have been a good thing.

I had lost the money and someone might have found it. They might have needed it. They might have kept it, even though it wasn't really theirs. (Finders keepers...) But it wasn't really mine either. It would have been *their* lucky day.

I don't believe in luck, or chance, or coincidences. I believe in God-incidences and as Psalm 139:16 says, "Every day of my life was recorded in your book. Every moment was laid out before a single day had passed."

Jesus came. Jesus died. Jesus rose. Jesus lives. Not by luck, not by chance, but by the will of God. He came for you. He came for me. His deepest desire is that you would begin a relationship with Him. Accept His love, His grace, and His mercy and enter in.

✓ REALITY CHECK

What are you holding on to that has no eternal value? Are your treasures in a box in the garage or stored up in heaven? How would you answer the question, "What must I do to receive eternal life?" And could you do it?

☒ PRAYER PAUSE

Father, in You alone I put my trust, my hope, and my future. Help me take my eyes off my earthly treasures and focus on eternal treasures. Earthly treasures are fleeting; we can't take them with us. Lord, my desire is to seek Your kingdom

Your Word says, "Do not store up for yourselves treasures on earth, where moth and rust destroy, and where thieves break in and steal. But store up for yourselves treasures in heaven, where moth and rust do not destroy, and where thieves do not break in and steal. For where your treasure is, there your heart will be also" (Matthew 6:19–21 NIV).

"But seek first his kingdom and his righteousness, and all these things will be given to you as well" (Matthew 6:33 NIV).

SOW WHAT?

I had credit for a flight on Southwest Airlines, thanks to a nasty bout with vertigo in which I'd had to cancel a flight to Oakland. Time was running out on the 12-month credit, and I was at the "use it or lose" it point.

So I offered the ticket up to anyone who wanted me to speak at an event—anywhere that Southwest flew from Portland, and they had to make up the difference in the cost of the flight if it was more than the value of my credit.

I was delighted when my friend Rachel Eggum Cinader jumped on the opportunity. She lives in Arizona, where it is warm. I live in Washington State where, well, the weather changes fast. Need I say more?

She told me she was putting together a convention for Hope for Women International and Dress a Girl Around the World, of which she is the founder and president. Not only that, I'd be staying with her and she has horses! Again, need I say more?

This had to be God-orchestrated because I have to tell you that being at a convention with a bunch of women who sew, for me, is laughable. My friends *did* laugh when I told them. God did not call me to be a *sewer* of fabric. Far from it! However, He did called me to be a *sower* of His Word.

My first encounter with the enemy came from my limited sewing experiences. I know full well where the enemy resides. I've experienced his torture many times, from about age 10 to 15. At 16, I learned how to fight him.

You see, the enemy resides under a sliding silver steel plate on a sewing machine. My grandma tried to teach me how to sew. Forget it. My patience at all the prep work was in short supply. In eighth and ninth grade I was required to take Home Economics and sewing was part of it. I probably hold the record for how many times a zipper had to be ripped out, leaving the skirt a size smaller due to lack of undamaged material. To this day, I remember the material was called Indian something or other, and it was red.

It was during those agonizing times that the enemy emerged in my life. The enemy has a name too. Bobbin. Bob-in. Only in my experience it was Bob-out! Bob never liked to stay hidden when I was around. Did you know that Bob can fly across the room at any given moment? Take my word for it. Or that Bob can make itself into a birds nest in its hidden home? Again, take my word for it.

I cheated in ninth grade. The project was to make a skirt, yes the skirt I ripped the zipper out of countless times, and model it at the Mother-Daughter Tea. I was "sick" the day of the tea. The next time we had to make something for a presentation, I took it home and had my grandma make it. There! I've confessed. I feel so much better.

Since Home Ec. was more than sewing, I passed! For my final project, I brought in an old canvas window shade, the kind you pull down, then pull down again, let it go, and watch it fly back up! During class, I used oil paintings to create a scene of mountains, a river and a brick wall. Hey! It was home décor! Our girls' physical education teacher had a window in her office that looked out on the gym, so I gave this to her to cover up the window. No more peeping Toms and Tammys.

When I reached the tenth grade, Home Ec. was no longer required.

Bring on P.E! Finally, my field of expertise! Let the games begin!

So what have I learned from my encounters with "Bob?" First Peter 5:8 says, "Be careful! Watch out for attacks from the Devil, your great enemy. He prowls around like a roaring lion, looking for some victim to devour."

I felt like a failure during the sewing section of Home Ec. Others seems to master the sewing, but not me. And as I look back on this disastrous time in my life, I'm reminded that what is important is who I am, not what I do. What I *do*, flows out of Whose I *am*. Form follows function.

I am loved by a Father who thinks I am fabulous! As I am loved, I love others. God loves us, we love God, and from that love, we love others. "'You must love the Lord your God with all your heart, all your soul, all your strength, and all your mind.' And, 'Love your neighbor as yourself'" (Luke 10:27). The Dress a Girl ladies are doing just that—loving God and loving His people.

I'm drawn to the story in 1 Corinthians 3:6-8: "My job was to plant the seed in your hearts, and Apollos watered it, but it was God, not we, who made it grow. The ones who do the planting or watering aren't important, but God is important because he is the one who makes the seed grow. The one who plants and the one who waters work as a team with the same purpose."

That verse is so freeing! I don't have to do it all! We are all called to *sow* seeds of God's love, but only God can make that love take root and grow. Through their *sewing*, the ladies I spoke with that weekend also *sowed*. I don't sew, but I can appreciate and encourage those who do.

God calls us to sow, to share His Word. Sometimes our job is to prepare the soil, or water it, or harvest the crop (Mark 4:1-20). Do what you were called to do. This is a team effort. But remember this: It is God who makes the seeds we plant grow. He gets the glory!

"And I am sure that God, who began the good work within you, will continue his work until it is finally finished on the day when Christ Jesus comes back again" (Philippians 1:6).

When God starts a project, He sees it through, unlike me with my sewing. So, sow on (or sew on!).

✓ REALITY CHECK

Galatians 6:7 says, "You will always reap what you sow!" How are you doing? Check what you've planted. Are you planting love, joy, peace, patience, kindness, goodness, faithfulness, gentleness, self-control? (See Galatians 5:22–23.)

⧗ PRAYER PAUSE

Jesus, Hosea 10:12 says, "Plant the good seeds of righteousness, and you will harvest a crop of my love." Help me be a sower of Your love, whether I prepare the field, plant the seed, water the soil, or bring in the harvest. Help me work together with others to do Your work. And may all the glory be Yours.

FOR FURTHER READING

Read Mark 4:1–20, the parable of the farmer scattering seed.

For more information on Hope for Women International/Dress a Girl Around the World and A Place to Dream: www.h4wi.org

THE ROCK

I'm not as agile as I used to be. So there, I admit it. I've had to give up leaping tall building at a single bound. Jumping off anything higher than three feet is now a no-no. My back, my knees or my ankles probably wouldn't hold up. Just walking on rocks along the seashore, I'm looking down for sure footing. Once glance up, I could fall. The water wouldn't be the only thing crashing on the shoreline.

Nothing is constant—the tide comes in and the tide goes out, pushed and pulled by the forces of nature. Life seems to be like that sometimes. The tide of our lives rushes onto the shore, covering the rocks, and hitting the retaining wall. We feel filled to the brim. As soon as we are filled, the tide starts out again. Back and forth goes life. It's gradual, like the tides.

The tides are a reminder for me. When the tide is in, it covers everything on the shore—sand, rocks, crabs, oysters, starfish, barnacles—everything. With the incoming tide, comes the seaweed and branches from trees. With the outgoing tide, everything that was covered, remains. Some of the seaweed is caught up in the rocks, but for the most part, it flows back with the tide.

In Cannon Beach, Oregon, there is a popular rock that tourists (and seagulls) "flock" to appropriately called Haystack Rock. It is a huge rock that stands tall and steady at the ocean's edge and looks like a large haystack. Every time I head to this coastal town, I make it a point to walk along the shore to the rock. It's an imposing sight, never moving, yet always changing. Something in my spirit leaps the minute I hit the beach and catch sight of it. As I walk, I keep my eyes on the rock. It appears to get bigger and bigger the closer I get.

As constant as the landmark is, the only constant in our lives is Jesus Christ. He is the Rock that will never trip us up. He asks us to look up; look to Him.

✓ REALITY CHECK

Do you have a constant in your life? May I suggest turning your eyes to Jesus?

⧖ PRAYER PAUSE

Lord God, I need You. Life seems to be like the tides at times: it flows in and out, has highs and lows, and is calm or angry. Jesus, thank You that You never change! You are the Rock of my Salvation and I will sing Your praises all the days of my life.

FINAL THOUGHTS

I sat in church on Easter Sunday taking notes—not about the sermon (sorry, Dave)—but about how to put an Amen to this book.

As I reflect back on the stories in this book, I'm reminded of the stone that was rolled away that Easter morning. His followers thought it was over—He was dead—when in fact, "it" was just beginning.

My questions to you, my friends, are these: What stone needs to be rolled away in your life to set you free? And what do you do when it is rolled away? Stay in the tomb, afraid to come out? Wait for someone to come in and get you? Or joyfully rush out?

God has rolled away the stone in your life. The stone of feeling less than, of being told you couldn't do something, and of feeling like you don't measure up. The stone of loss, of despair, and of feeling trapped. Do you have a past that haunts you, mistakes you've made, and you think you will never get past them? You have been set free! Now go and live like it! There is freedom in Christ. He paid the penalty so you and I would not have to live like slaves, but as free people. "It is for freedom that Christ has set us free. Stand firm, then, and do not let yourselves be burdened again by a yoke of slavery" (Galatians 5:1 NIV).

Can I get a *loud* AMEN!

TO ORDER
ADDITIONAL COPIES OF

Every Time I Turn Around,
God Whispers in My Ear!

OR HER OTHER BOOKS:

Every Time I Turn Around, I Bump into God!
Every Time I Turn Around, I Catch a Glimpse of God!

Send $13.99 plus $2.00 shipping (USA) to:
Barb Boswell
P.O. Box 578
Woodland, WA 98674

Or order online at: www.barbboswell.com
and click on "shopping mall."

*Mail order, please indicate which books you are ordering.

For information regarding having Barb speak at
your event, contact her at bbos2@juno.com